Marriage in Paradise

*How to Have a Genesis Two Marriage
in a Genesis Three World.*

William P. Farley

"This book has been written from the perspective of a man who has been married more than 47 years, parented five children, studied and preached the biblical texts on marriage, and counseled countless couples about their marriages. In other words, this book isn't a theoretical approach to marriage; rather it contains the practical wisdom of almost a half-a-century of learning and living God's design for the union of a man and woman. I cannot imagine any marriage that wouldn't benefit from this book." *Donald S. Whitney, Professor of Biblical Spirituality and Associate Dean, The Southern Baptist Theological Seminary, Louisville, KY. Author of Spiritual Disciplines for the Christian Life, Praying the Bible, and Family Worship.*

"Not many books on marriage quote both theologian Abraham Kuyper and musical artist Paul Simon in their introduction. But this juxtaposition of sources illustrates Bill Farley's passion to demonstrate how a robust, gospel-centered theology of marriage challenges the messages from popular culture that far too often impoverish the husband and wife relationship. I hope and pray that this book gets a wide reading so that God's wise and loving design for marriage is both understood more accurately and practiced more faithfully, for our good and for His glory." *Randal Roberts, President and Professor of Christian Spirituality, Western Seminary (Portland, OR)*

"In *Marriage in Paradise*, William Farley combines a solid biblical exposition of marriage with easy to follow application steps, designed to help the reader get the gospel back into the center of their marriage. In a world full of dysfunctional marriages, pastors should keep half-dozen copies of *Marriage in Paradise* on their bookshelf to give away – it's that helpful." *Marty Machowski, pastor, and author of Parenting First Aid, The Ology, Long Story Short, and other gospel-rich books and resources for church and home.*

"Bill and Judy have been married for nearly 50 years, which makes me want to listen and learn. This is a book about God and marriage that is both biblical and helpful, whether you are single, engaged or have been married for many years. It has the theological depth that will challenge you and practical advice to help spur on good conversations, pointing you not toward having a perfect marriage, but a Christ-centered, God-glorifying one." *Darren Carlson, Ph.D., President, Training Leaders International*

"William Farley writes about "how to have a Genesis 2 marriage in a Genesis 3 world." Translation: how do we live as God designed marriage to be in a world that is destroying marriage? And the answer: we believe God's good news for a fallen world--the gospel! Sound too simple? Before you make that assumption, read Farley's explanation of the "implications of the gospel for marriage." Turns out the gospel is exactly what we need to hear, believe and live. This book comes from the heart of a husband, father, and pastor and is theologically based and filled with cases and valuable resources. I'm happy to recommend this important book." *Stephen Smallman, Pastor, author of The Walk, Forty Days on the Mountain, Spiritual Birth Line, etc.*

©2018 William P. Farley

All rights reserved. No part of this book may be reproduced, stored, in a retrieval system, or transmitted in any form or by any means—electronic, mechanical, photocopy, recording, or otherwise—except for brief quotations for the purpose of review or comment, without the prior permission from the author in writing. He can be contacted at 8827 S. Cliffview Lane, Spokane, WA. 99224, or by email at bfarley48@gmail.com

Unless otherwise indicated, Scripture quotations are from *ESV Bible* ® (*The Holy Bible, English Standard Version*®). Copyright ©2001 Crossway Bibles., a publishing ministry of Good News Publishers. Used by permission. All rights reserved.

ISBN: 9781727156836

Printed in the United States of America

The characters, places, and incidents in this book are a product of my personal pastoral experience. Most are a combination of the mixing and melding of several stories over time. However, I have sufficiently changed the names and circumstances to protect the identity of the original people involved.

First printing Fall 2018.

Cover Design by Sarah Mikucki… Sarah@doorpostdesigns.co

WILLIAM FARLEY WAS CONVERTED to Christ in 1971 while doing graduate studies at Gonzaga University. He worked for 25 years in the business world while actively participating as a lay elder in his church. He retired from his business in 1998 to write. In 2002 he planted a church, Grace Christian Fellowship. It has grown to become one church with two campuses.

In March of 2018 he passed the baton of leadership to his oldest son, who is also a pastor, and retired. He continues to write, speak at conferences and encourage church planters wherever he finds them. He has been married to his wife, Judy, for 47 years. They have five children and twenty-two grandchildren. Bill's writing experience includes the following:

- *Outrageous Mercy* (Baker Books, 2004, republished by (P&R 2009)
- *Gospel Powered Parenting,* (P&R 2009)
- *Gospel Powered Humility* (P&R 2011) *World Magazine's* runner up books of the year.
- *Hidden in the Gospel* (P&R 2014)
- *The Secret to Spiritual Joy* (Cruciform 2015).
- He has written for *Discipleship Journal, Enrichment Journal,* (a national pastor's magazine); *Focus on The Family Magazine, Pulpit Helps, The Journal of Biblical Counseling, Reformation 21,* and the *Spokesman Review.*
- His article, *God's Highest Passion,* was honored in the Evangelical Press Association's biblical exposition category.

Introduction	i
ONE: Marriage in Paradise	1
TWO: A Politically Incorrect Paradise	17
THREE: Paradise Lost	35
FOUR: Paradise Restored	47
FIVE: The Gospel	65
SIX: Surpassing Knowledge	77
SEVEN: The School of Christ	89
EIGHT: Gospel Humility	101
NINE: Ambition?	117
TEN: Three Last Questions	127
ELEVEN: Best Friends for Life	141
TWELVE: Building on the Foundation	153
THIRTEEN: God's Super Glue	171
FOURTEEN: God's Dump Truck	187
Endnotes	191

Introduction

EVERY BOOK ON MARRIAGE gives off an aroma. It reflects the author's experience. When the writer's marriage has been lackluster or even unhappy, the odor is endurance. Marriage is a duty. Gird up your loins. Persevere. Finish the race. A better marriage is coming.

But when the author's marriage has been positive, when the author has tasted the joys that God created marriage to provide, the pages celebrate joy. It is the sweet aroma of gratitude, and hope for an even better marriage in this life and in the eternity to come.

This writer falls in the latter category. I have been delightfully and happily married since 1971. Judy and I have known the normal ups and downs of sleeping, eating, and raising children with another fallen creature. We know what relational bruises feel like. But, if knowing what I know today, I had the opportunity to marry her again, I would be even more excited than I was on my wedding day. I have no regrets.

Why have we been so happy? We have both wholeheartedly, but imperfectly, sought to live out the implications of the gospel for marriage. I have written this book to share that joy with you.

However, the experience of many has not been this positive. We are all sinners. The title of Bob Dylan's song, "Everything Is Broken," says it well. We live in a fallen world. At some level, all relationships are "broken." But I want to convince you that, despite our fallenness, God has something better than the daily grind of pedantic perseverance.

Our marriage is a display of God's amazing grace transforming two unworthy sinners. I was converted three months after our wedding—Judy a year later. But shortly after our conversion, God gave us faith to believe that those who die to self will become increasingly happy. This principle applies to all of life, but especially to marriage.

Make no mistake; God has wired each of us to pursue our happiness, and we will ruthlessly and single-mindedly pursue it by doing whatever we *really* believe will get us there.

That is one of the fruits of new birth. It convinces us that our ultimate happiness is in God and eternal things. To the degree that we really believe this we will push self, deny self, humble self, and even suffer, to possess that happiness. The pursuit of that joy is what Jesus had in mind when he said, "Whoever would save his life will lose it, but whoever loses his life for my sake will find it" (Matthew 10:39, 16:25). At the cross Jesus practiced what he taught. "For the joy set before him [he] endured the cross" (Hebrew 12:2).

We can restate it like this: Those willing to die to their selfish me-centeredness will wake up one day to discover that they are maximizing their marital joy.

These words are counter intuitive. Obeying them is not easy. Everything in our fallen nature thinks the opposite—

You gain your life by protecting it.

Happiness comes through self-promotion.

Successful people protect their reputations. They don't lose them.

Introduction

Real happiness comes to those who excel at taking care of number one. You never volunteer to be number two.

Here is the language that expresses these assumptions.

"I'm not going to let you use me. I have my rights, you know."

"I will do my part for this marriage if you do yours."

"After what you have done to me, do you really expect me to forgive?"

"How could anyone ever thank God for a spouse like you? God knows I deserve better."

However, these words, and others, express the kind of thinking that leads to marital pain not joy.

So, here is the question: do we believe Jesus? Those who do pursue their joy in the happiness of their spouse. Here is a simple, but profound, truth: if a husband and wife truly understand, and apply the ethic of the cross to their marriage, they can't help but become increasingly happy. As someone once said, *two funerals precede every happy and successful marriage.*

That is the point of this book. I want to convince you that the ethic of the cross stands at the center of every truly fulfilling marriage. The cross does three things. It teaches husband and wife *how* to love each other—first as spouses, and then as brothers and sisters. Second, it *motivates* that love. Third, because it lavishes us with buckets of grace when we fail, it encourages us to keep walking the steady path of self-denial.

THE BIBLE IS SUFFICIENT

There are many Christian books on marriage in print. Why a new one? I have four reasons. First, I am completely convinced that the Bible is sufficient to transform your marriage into a rewarding, satisfying, and God-glorifying union. You don't need the latest book on therapy. In fact, the therapeutic movement is often contrary to biblical teaching. You don't need most secular self-help books. Some might even make things worse. You need nothing but the Bible, prayer, and a gospel-centered, Bible-believing church. This assumption is the first way this book is different.

MARRIED LOVE IS UNIQUE

There is a second reason for this book. How the Bible commands husbands and wives to love each other is unique. Christian couples love each other *structurally*, in a hierarchy of headship and submission. But, they also love each other *personally*—as friends and lovers—with tenderness, affection, humility, and servanthood. Last, they love each other *sexually*. Not enough books on Christian marriage make these distinctions. Many focus on how spouses love each other personally, or sexually, but give lip service to how they should love each other structurally. Few sufficiently emphasize *both* the structural and personal aspects of marriage.

I recently attended a marriage conference. The speaker, a well-known evangelical author, gave five lectures on marriage to about 250 couples. The content was biblical. He covered important subjects like living sacrificially, forgiving each other, the need to work at communication, etc. In general, I believe his talks helped those listening.

What concerned me was what he didn't mention. First, he didn't relate his ethical teaching back to the cross. This matters because the cross is the model and motivation for all Christian ethics, especially marriage. Second, He didn't talk about the all-important subject of God's structural purpose for marriage—one of the crucial ways married love differs from the way we love other people.

The first half of this book will discuss the structural aspects of marital love. The second half will explore how to love each other personally. The last chapter will talk about sex. Happy marriages excel at all three.

THE CENTRALITY OF THE CROSS

A third reason for this book is the need for a book on marriage with the cross at its center. The cross stands at the center of the gospel, and throughout history, to the degree that a revival of cross-centeredness has occurred, there has also been a revival of biblical marriage. The two are inseparable.

The 16th century Reformation is a good example. Martin Luther's biographer, Roland Bainton, notes that Luther's marriage to Katie von Bora set the tone for German marriage for the next four hundred years.[1]

In the same way, 17th century English Puritanism continued that focus, and J.I. Packer notes how the Puritan marital ideal also became the standard by which the English measured their marriages for the next three hundred years.[2]

For this reason, chapter five and six are all about the gospel. The theology of the cross is infinitely deep. It is a well with no bottom. I presume that most of my readers are Christians, but I also presume that, no matter how long you have been a believer, your knowledge of the cross needs to go deeper. Last, I presume that your marriage will only go as deep as your understanding of Christ's atoning work on the cross. As we have already noted, the cross shows us what love looks like. It motivates us to try. And it is the source of God's grace when we fail.

MARRIAGE MATTERS

Fourth, I have written this because the institution of marriage is dying. Progressives assume that traditional marriage is dispensable. After all, aren't there many valid living arrangements? TV ads and social discourse now use "partner" instead of spouse. But, if the Bible is right, this way of thinking will ultimately prove exceedingly costly.

MARRIAGE IN PARADISE

The strong-force holds the nucleus of the atom together. No one knows how it works, but we do know that if it ceases its binding work, the entire universe will dissolve into random chaos. In the same way, the marital covenant is the "strong-force" that holds human culture together. To the degree that we weaken or dishonor it, the social order will also eventually unravel.

Another way to say this is that marriage is the fundamental social institution. It was the only institution created by God prior to the Fall. Abraham Kuyper has argued that the others—civil government, educational institutions, armies, etc.—have come into existence *because* of the Fall.[3] In other words, had there been no sin, there would probably be no need for civil government or armies. But marriage is different. It is the one social institution without which we cannot thrive.

Not only is marriage important because it is central to the social order, but it matters because God loves it. The Bible opens and closes with a wedding. In Genesis 2 God united Adam and Eve in a one-flesh union. It was the first wedding. But, Revelation 21 concludes the Bible with a greater wedding—that of Christ to his Bride, the Church.

These facts emphasize the need to prioritize Ephesians 5:32 where Paul informs us that the wedding of Christ to his church is primary. It is eternal. The wedding of Adam and Eve is important, but it is temporal (See Matthew 22:30). God united Adam and Eve to point us to Christ and his church, to make that wedding look good, to create in us a longing for its ultimate fulfillment.

As Christ's bride, the church, submits to him, so God asks each wife to submit to her husband, encouraging and respecting his leadership (Ephesians 5:22-24, 33).

Christ loves his Bride, the church. He serves her extravagantly. He went to the cross and suffered horribly to

Introduction

redeem her. In the same way, God commands each husband to imitate Christ's sacrificial love by the way he loves his own wife (Ephesians 5:25-33).

It is seldom recognized that the husband has the harder assignment. In the inimitable words of C.S. Lewis, a husband's "headship...is most fully embodied... in him whose marriage is most *like a crucifixion*; whose wife receives most and gives least, is most unworthy of him, is—in her own mere nature—least lovable."[4]

We should also note that, whenever the New Testament Apostles write about *how* God wants married couples to relate, they don't talk about communication. They don't discuss sex, relating to in-laws, or the importance of keeping a budget. Instead, they always return to governmental order. There are only four texts, and they all emphasize the same truth. (See 1 Corinthians 11:2-3, Ephesians 5:22-33, Colossians 3:18-19, and 1 Peter 3:1-7). Husbands lead your wives by loving and love your wives by leading. Wives, encourage, and submit to his leadership. Since that is the biblical emphasis, it should also be ours. Governmental order should not be an embarrassing after-thought.

Of course, anyone that has been married for more than a few weeks knows that governmental order is just the beginning. It is not the totality. In the words of Paul Simon, marriage is the mingling of "hearts and bones." It is the only relationship that fuses expectations of romance and affection with hierarchical order. We go to bed and wake up next to a fellow Christian, and we are commanded to love that other person as Christ has loved us (John 15:12). Martin Luther noted that the Bible commands us to love our brother and sister. Katie [his wife] was his closest sister. Therefore, he confessed that she needed to be the first object of his love. In other words, his love for Katie was a proving ground. How he served her, forgave her, spoke to her, encouraged her, listened to her, and honored her was the litmus test of his spiritual authenticity.

Here is the bottom line: marriage tests our ability to love. That is because your spouse is the one person who knows your strengths and weaknesses better than anyone else. They can use that power to abuse you. But, because no one really sees how we relate in private, he or she is also the easiest person to look down on, use, or abuse.

In high school chemistry we dipped litmus paper into solutions to test their acidity or alkalinity. Red meant acidic, blue meant alkaline. In the same way, what really goes on in your marriage is a litmus test. It measures your spiritual maturity, the strength of your faith, and how deeply the gospel has affected you. How a husband serves, how his wife encourages his leadership, the depth of their mutual humility and growing friendship is God's litmus test. Their sexual relationship is the frosting that sweetens the cake.

There is a problem: you can fake it. At church, and other social settings, you can put on an outward show and look like the perfect couple, but when the front door is closed, the world is outside, and it's just you and kids inside, what really goes on? Maybe something completely different. No one knows but God, the angels, and your children.

Andrew Fuller was the 18th century pastor-theologian who raised money to support William Carey on the mission field. About Andrew Fuller, his son, Andrew Gunton Fuller (1799–1884) wrote these powerful words of praise. "There is no division of a man's life so marked and characteristic as that which is made by the door of his own house, on the two sides of which are witnessed sometimes two distinct men, and always two distinct phases of character which act and react on each other."[5] Then he went on to describe the consistency, the lack of hypocrisy, that characterized his father. *"My father was the same on both sides of the door."*

Are you and I the same on both sides of the door? Although they will never tell you, our children are watching. They alone know, and the fruits of our authenticity will be apparent to all when they enter their adult years.

In addition, because we need their love more than any other person, our spouse has the greatest power to hurt us. "Hatred was never so powerful as when it exists between two spouses," Luther observed.[6] That is because our spouse is at times the hardest person to love, and at other times, the easiest. For this reason, marriage is where the spiritual rubber meets the road of life. It is God's spiritual litmus paper.

SPIRITUAL WARFARE

Since such great outcomes ride on marriage, it should not surprise us that it is the focal point of contemporary spiritual warfare. In fact, the first spiritual warfare occurred in Genesis 3, and amongst other things, it was a devastating attack on marriage. The Devil subverted the divine order that God created Adam and Eve to express. We will see how he started with Eve and then worked his way up the chain of command to Adam, and then to God. The modern world scorns the idea of a wife submitting. What could be more politically incorrect? The command for a husband to love sacrificially is also ignored. So is the concept of a husband and wife complimenting each other with different skills and roles.

This means any couple who wants to experience a biblical marriage will need to swim upstream, against powerful cultural pressures. But, because God commands us to make the effort, true Christians will not waver in their resolve.

For those willing to read this book I have better expectations. My wife and I want to infect your marriage, the marriages of those around you, and the marriages of your children and grandchildren with a contagious joy, a joy that is the fruit of marriage centered on Christ *through* his gospel.

MARRIAGE IN PARADISE

The 19th century literary figure, Ambrose Bierce, summed it up well.

> Marriage is a community consisting of a master, a mistress, and *two slaves*, making in all, one person.

And Ray Ortlund concludes—

> The only arrangement for sex and marriage that has any chance of working today is that which moves toward restoring our Edenic origins. If we modern Western egalitarians can hold our emotional horses long enough to imagine how a woman might be dignified by helping a worthy man who loves her sacrificially, as both the man and the woman humbly pursue the glory of God together, the profile of man and woman that blessed us in Eden will start looking more plausible as an approach to human happiness today.[7]

With these quotes as a segue, we turn to the first chapter, a study of the first marriage. The wedding took place in a Genesis two paradise. Before we do that, an important note. This book contains the stories of many couples. In every case the names and circumstances have been changed to protect their identities. Sometimes the story is a combination of several couple's experiences. At other times it is half true and part fictional. All are the byproduct of many decades of pastoral experience.

ONE: Marriage in Paradise

SEVERAL YEARS AGO, I was blessed to travel to Hawaii for vacation. We spent a week on the Island of Maui. The main village is a 19th century whaling town named Lahaina. Cheeseburgers in Paradise, a restaurant that I remember with great fondness, was on the second floor of an old waterfront building.

In terms of weather, Hawaii is a paradise. The temperature rarely rises above eighty-five or falls below sixty-five. In fact, it was so temperate that Cheeseburgers in Paradise had screens instead of windows. That night it was full of sunburned mainlanders eating cheeseburgers, sipping their favorite beverage, and relaxing. The sun set as warm tropical breezes blew through the open screens.

It was a special moment.

This chapter is not about cheeseburgers. It is about marriage, but it shares something in common with cheeseburgers—the word, "paradise." It is about marriage in paradise. It is about the inner workings of the male-female relationship that God intended. These relationships we often take for granted, but they are absolutely central to all that goes on in the real world. Healthy churches and cultures celebrate and encourage the differences between the sexes. That is because human flourishing, and the glory of God, rises and falls on how men and women relate. On the shoulders of this interaction rides the fate of civilizations.

The point of this chapter is that God intended marriage to be wonderful in a way that our sin-saturated minds cannot imagine. The Bible describes this union in Genesis 1 and 2. It was the first marriage, and it was in paradise.

By biblical standards our expectations for marriage are often substandard. The social sciences remind us that, even in a fallen world, married people are happier than singles. A 2005 survey funded by the Pew Charitable Trust showed that "Forty-three percent of married respondents reported that they were 'very happy,' compared to 24 percent of unmarried individuals. The results were consistent for all age groups and genders."[1] In another study of three thousand women, fifty percent of those who were married reported that they were very happy. Only twenty-five percent of those who were single could say the same.[2]

Married people are also healthier and live longer. According to the Center for Disease Control married people drink and smoke less, experience fewer headaches and psychological problems.

Married people have more money. Married men earn more than single men doing the same job. This phenomenon is so pronounced that sociologists call it the "marriage premium." According to one study, "Married men work about 400 hours more and make about $16,000 more per year than a single in the same job, and they are less likely to quit without lining up a new one."[3] Tim Keller observes that "individuals who were continuously married had 75 percent more wealth at retirement than those who never married or who divorced and did not remarry."[4] George Gilder suggested the obvious. If faced with a choice between getting a college degree or getting married, a man will probably earn more if he gets married than by going to college and remaining single.

Not only is it true that married people are happier, healthier, and wealthier than singles, but it is also true that a marriage that revolves around Christ will be happier than one that does not. When people say that God is at the center of their marriage, satisfaction levels rise another twenty-five percent.[5] A God-centered marriage also reduces the probability of divorce. In a fifteen-year U.S. study, thirty-seven percent of couples who rarely or never attended a religious service had divorced, whereas only fourteen percent of couples who attended church together on a regular basis had experienced divorce.[6] According to Shaunti Feldhahn, "the rate of divorce in the church is 25 to 50 percent lower than among those who don't attend worship services, and those who prioritize their faith and/or pray together are dramatically happier and more connected than those who don't."[7]

This should not surprise us. God created Adam and Eve to experience an unfettered paradise in their relationship. The 17th century Puritans might seem like a strange model, but they took God's expectations for Christian marriage seriously. In his book, *Worldly Saints,* Leland Ryken quotes Cotton Mather, who "called his second wife 'a most lovely creature and such a gift of Heaven to me and mine that the sense thereof…dissolves me into tears of joy.'"

Another 17th century Puritan pastor, Thomas Hooker wrote, "The man whose heart is endeared to the woman he loves…dreams of her in the night, hath her in his eye and apprehension when he awakes, museth on her as he sits at the table, walks with her when he travels…she lies in his bosom, and his heart trusts in her, which forceth all to confess that the stream of his affection, like a mighty current, runs with full tide and strength."[8]

MARRIAGE IN PARADISE

The English Puritan, Thomas Gataker, wrote, "There is no society more near, more entire, more needful, more kindly, more delightful, more comfortable, more constant, more continual, than the society of man and wife, the main root, source, and original of all other societies."[9] Martin Luther added, "The dearest life is to live with a godly, willing, obedient wife in peace and unity."[10] And, Edward Taylor, the 18th century New England Puritan minister and poet, wrote to his wife that his passion for her was a "golden ball of pure fire."[11]

I am not suggesting that a painless, stress less, no-conflict marriage is the biblical norm. We live in a fallen world, and we are fallen creatures. That explains why many do not experience this kind of happiness. One of the reports just cited indicates that only forty-three percent of married couples are "very happy." Why is this figure not seventy-five or eighty-five percent? The problem is selfishness— the heart and soul of sin. In addition, it is important to note that it is *your* indwelling sin, not your spouse's, that is usually the source of that angst. Therefore, there will always be some trouble.

But the opposite is also true. The more we pursue God's blueprint for marriage the more fulfilled and happy we will become. That is the biblical testimony. "An excellent wife is the crown of her husband" (Pr. 12:4). "She is far more precious than jewels" (Pr. 13:11). "He who finds a wife finds a good thing, and obtains favor from the Lord" (Pr. 18:22).

For those who would describe their marriage as "very happy," I have written this book to make it even happier. I have also written this book to protect you from the loss of that happiness.

Maybe you have a boring, routine marriage. The fizz is gone. You are not unhappy, but you are just going through the motions. Your marriage lacks passion. It is routine. I have written this book to pull you out of what a friend of mine called "the marriage doldrums."

Last, I have written this book for those who are struggling. Your relationship is a war interspersed with temporary truces. You are miserable. You have thought about divorce, but you are a Christian, and so you just soldier on. I have written this book to provide you with solutions, to give you hope. The solutions are not easy, and the results seldom come instantaneously, but when persistently applied long-term, they work miracles.

There are many contemporary cultural beliefs and values that conspire to destroy marital fulfillment. Feminism and the sexual revolution have profoundly crippled the relationships between the sexes. They have also impacted marriage. Some of the contemporary fruits are sexual promiscuity, a flood of single parenthood, a growing reluctance to marry, falling fertility rates, sex role confusion, and prolonged male adolescence. In the Western World, relationships between men and women are in an advanced stage of decay.

This chapter will discuss marriage as God originally designed it. God recorded that design in Genesis chapter 2. However, I must warn you. God's blueprint is counter-cultural. But it does have this glorious recommendation. It works! It *really* works! In addition, the happiness that people enjoy by following God's plan glorifies him. It makes God look good. Here are some of the crucial principles—

- God is our Creator. This means he has property rights over us. He makes the rules, and love motivates the rules that he makes.
- God's purpose for marriage is bigger than our personal happiness.
- He created two sexes, male and female. For his glory and our happiness, he made us different.
- God created men and women equal in dignity and value.
- God created men and women to fill distinct and different marital roles.

- God created marriage to allow us to share in the joy of children.
- God designed marriage to be a life-long relationship between one man and one woman.
- God created marriage to be the normal state for adults.

In all of this God had two ends in mind. First, glory for himself, second, human fulfillment through God's plan for marriage, sexuality, and true marital love.

GOD IS OUR CREATOR

The first step back to paradise occurs when we honor and celebrate God as our Creator. Because God created man and woman, and the paradise in which he placed us, he is Lord of that paradise. The act of creation entitles him to Lordship.

> So God created man in his own image, in the image of God he created him; male and female he created them. And God blessed them. And God said to them, "Be fruitful and multiply and fill the earth and subdue it and have dominion over the fish of the sea and over the birds of the heavens and over every living thing that moves on the earth (Gen. 1:27-28).

Notice how the text begins, "So God *created* man" (Gen. 1:26). We did not create ourselves. We are not self-originating. Natural selection did not fashion us. We did not evolve from the primordial soup. God *created* us! God custom-spoke each human being into existence. God carefully assembles each person's DNA. He knits each person together in his or her mother's womb. We are all fearfully and wonderfully made (Psalm 139:5).

Creation also means ownership. By the act of creation God possesses the right of ownership. This means he makes the rules. He decides how men and women should relate. It also implies a day of final judgment when he will hold us accountable to those rules.

This is the question around which the culture wars revolve. Who makes the rules, God or man? If we are the byproduct of evolutionary chance then we are accountable to no one, and we are free to create our own rules. Pragmatism is our guiding ethic. Truth is whatever works.

But Christians serve a good and sovereign Creator. Christians delight in their creaturliness, and they submit to their Creator's lordship. Therefore, conversion is a glad entrance into our Creator's kingdom. Conversion means *joyful* submission to God's authority.

God's authority is not the starting point for Western culture. Increasingly, secular culture, and the modern individual, reject all authority outside of self. "The most fundamental belief in American culture," notes sociologist Robert Bellah, "is that moral truth is relative to individual consciousness."[12] It comes down to this: I create my own rules. Cultural observers call this narcissistic autonomy "expressive individualism."

This is not Christianity. Christian conversion is a decisive change. It means a rejection of "expressive individualism." It means that, when it comes to marriage, secular culture does not make the rules. Opinion polls do not make the rules. Government does not make the rules. Our educational system does not make the rules. The media does not make the rules. God makes the rules! In the words of Isaiah, "The LORD is our judge; the LORD is our lawgiver; the LORD is our king; he will save us" (Isaiah 33:22).

In any discussion about marriage, this must be the crucial starting point.

In addition, it also means that obedience is safe. This Rule Maker is infinitely good. He loves us. He makes rules to protect us and to maximize our happiness. God alone knows how to make relationships thrive. He designed Adam and Eve to work efficiently and happily. We are most apt to experience that happiness when we follow the Designer's manual.

Last, creation also means accountability. A Day of Judgment is coming "When, according to my gospel," Paul warns, "God judges the secrets of men by Christ Jesus" (Romans 2:16). On that day, we will wish we hadn't sung Frank Sinatra's song, "I did it my way." Why? Because "We must all appear before the judgment seat of Christ, so that each one may receive what is due for what he has done in the body, whether good or evil" (2 Corinthians 5:10).

In summary, we will enter God's marital paradise to the degree that we submit to our Creator's authority. Because he is infinitely good, his authority is safe. Ultimately, he will hold us accountable. Everything that follows rests upon this crucial assumption.

GOD'S PURPOSE FOR MARRIAGE

In the last few decades Western culture has changed its understanding of the purpose for marriage. Marriage used to be an institution honored by every culture. People married because they needed a life companion. They wanted a sexual relationship. But they also married to have children, to create a healthy environment in which to raise them, and to serve the larger culture. Marriage and children used to be a rite of passage into adulthood.

This understanding has changed. For the first time in history the broader culture views marriage selfishly. Legal scholar, John Witte, Jr., writes that "the earlier ideal of marriage as a permanent contractual union designed for the sake of mutual love, procreation, and protection is slowly giving way to a new reality of marriage as a *'terminal sexual contract'* designed for the gratification of the individual parties."[13]

But this was never God's purpose for marriage. God created marriage for his glory. God's glory is his moral beauty.

The angels, your friends, and your children should be able to look at your marriage and see a picture of God's moral beauty.

Specifically, God designed human marriage to display the moral beauty of the ultimate marriage—the one between Christ and his bride, the church. That is the message of Ephesians 5:32. "This mystery is profound, and I am saying that it refers to Christ and his church." The gospel made the marriage of Christ to his church possible. So ultimately our marriages exist to display the *fruit* of the gospel—Christ's reconciliation to, and love for, his bride the church.

There are also secondary reasons. God created marriage to produce children. "Be fruitful and multiply and fill the earth" (Gen. 1:28). God created marriage to meet our need for human companionship and relationship. "It is not good that man should be alone. I will make him a helper fit for him" (Gen 2:18). Last, he created it as an outlet for sexual desire. "But because of the temptation to sexual immorality, each man should have his own wife and each woman her own husband" (1 Corinthians 7:2).

This means that fulfilling God's purpose for marriage does not require children or health. You can be married and unable to have children, or you can be married and lack companionship because your spouse has Alzheimer's, but you can still make Christ's love for his church, and the church's glad submission to it, look gloriously attractive. In other words, you can still glorify God, and that is the ultimate reason for marriage.

In his book, *The Meaning of Sex,* theologian, Denny Burk sums it up this way: "The deepest meaning of marriage is that it is an enacted parable of another marriage— the marriage of Christ to his bride."[14]

TWO SEXES FOR GOD'S GLORY

In contemporary culture, the gender options are multiplying like rabbits. Besides male and female there is agender, cisgender, genderfluid, genderqueer, intersex, transgender, etc. But this does not describe God's paradise, and any attempts to circumvent God's gender options will terminate in misery.

God created only two sexes, and he created them for his glory. "Let us make man in our image...Male and female he created them" (Gen. 1:26, 27). In scripture, the "image" of God and the glory of God are synonyms. Therefore, created in God's "image and likeness" can be restated "created to reflect God's glory."[15] This means that God made only two sexes, and he made them different to magnify his glory and our happiness.

This should not surprise us. Equality expressing itself through diversity is God's modus operandi. The members of the Godhead—Father, Son, and Holy Spirit—are equal in value but different in function. In the same way, God created two sexes, male and female, also equal in value but different in function. He did this to display his nature, which is his glory. If this is true, our attempts to amplify the number of sexual options, while denying the innate differences between the sexes, is a direct attack on God's glory.

God loves the two sexes he created. He wants us to celebrate the uniqueness of each. That is why androgyny, and sex change operations are so offensive. They rebel against his right to assign a specific gender to each of us. They reject God's authority to be our creator.

What about the exceptions? A tiny fraction of people are born with a chromosomal defect that are called, "intersexed." That means they have both male and female genitals, or some combination thereof. Our compassion runs deep for those with this condition. In many cases, modern surgery can reverse the effects. The percent born this way is small—anywhere from 1 in 1,000 to 1 in 10,000, depending upon the specific intersexed condition.[16]

The sexual revolutionaries use this to argue that gender is fluid—that there are more than two sexual options. But it is always a mistake to argue from the exception to the norm. We wouldn't use the albino condition to argue that there is no such thing as normal human skin pigmentation. We shouldn't do that with sex either. The intersexed condition is a genetic abnormality, not a genetic norm.

EQUAL IN VALUE

Most people think that Christianity oppresses women and liberates men. The truth is the exact opposite. Christianity elevates the status of women. Of all the world religions it alone gives women equal status with men. How do non-Christian cultures treat women? Buddhist, Shinto, and Hindu cultures take pride in denying women equality with men. Islam is the poster-child for this principle. The image of burka-clad women, walking with eyes downcast, unable to obtain a driver's license, treated like chattel, walking ten feet behind their husbands, says it all.

Secularism, like Christianity's other competitors, also oppresses women, and secularism is increasingly the religion of the West. It doesn't oppress by prohibiting equal opportunity. It oppresses by denying the God given differences between men and women. The fruits are the enslavement of women in a different direction. The family responsibilities that God created men to assume get transferred to their wives. Newly liberated, she not only cares for the house and children, but also is a breadwinner. *Time Magazine* observes the following.

> As women have gained more freedom, more education and more economic power, they have become less happy. 'No tidy theory explains the trend,' notes University of Pennsylvania economist Justin Wolfers, a co-author of *The Paradox of Declining Female*

MARRIAGE IN PARADISE

> *Happiness.* 'We looked across all sectors — young vs. old, kids or no kids, married or not married, education, no education, working or not working — and it stayed the same.'[17]

The reality is the opposite. Feminism doesn't liberate women; it enslaves them. It liberates men. It liberates men from the responsibility to lead, provide for, and protect women and children.

God's Genesis 2 blueprint liberates both men and women. It starts with the truth that God created men and women equal in value, equal in worth, and equal in dignity.

> Then the LORD God said, "It is not good that the man should be alone; I will make him a *helper* fit for him." Now out of the ground the LORD God had formed every beast of the field and every bird of the heavens and brought them to the man to see what he would call them. And whatever the man called every living creature, that was its name. The man gave names to all livestock and to the birds of the heavens and to every beast of the field. But for Adam there was not found a helper fit for him. So the LORD God caused a deep sleep to fall upon the man, and while he slept took one of his ribs and closed up its place with flesh. And the rib that the LORD God had taken from the man he made into a woman and brought her to the man. Then the man said, "This at last is bone of my bones and flesh of my flesh; she shall be called Woman, because she was taken out of Man." Therefore, a man shall leave his father and his mother and hold fast to his wife, and they shall become one flesh. And the man and his wife were both naked and were not ashamed (Genesis 2:18–25).

The term, "equal in value" means that God created Adam and Eve with equal access to the grace of God, equal access to a relationship with God, and equal opportunity to reflect the glory of God. In other words, he created both sexes in his image. Ontology is a big word. It means the nature of a thing. In philosophical terms, God created Adam and Eve ontologically equal.

God's presentation of the animals to Adam to be his helper makes this clear. Why did Adam reject the animals? He was looking for an *ontological equal*, and the animals were ontologically inferior. Adam treated the animals like the Islamic world treats its women. He rejected them. They were not his equal. But Adam treated Eve like no other religion treats women. He loved her, served her, and honored her.

A beautiful picture of Eve's equality occurs at her creation. Although God created Adam from the ground, from dirt, he created Eve from *Adam's side.* He did this to emphasize her unique status. In the words of Puritan Bible commentator, Matthew Henry, she was not created from his head to Lord it over him, nor from his feet so that he could lord it over her. Instead, God took her from Adam's side, from a bone over his heart, as a sign of Adam's love and care for her, to signify that she was his equal, his companion, his beloved, his delight, and his friend.

All of this occurred in an atmosphere free from guilt and shame. It occurred in an environment of love, tenderness, intimacy, and mutual serving. Some women read romance novels to fill the void in their hearts created by the absence of this kind of relationship. God created Eve to be the object of Adam's tenderness. In other words, God created Adam and Eve to share his unblemished love in a permanent, monogamous relationship of joy and love.

SUMMARY

Are your expectations for marriage too low? God has more, but to access it we need to submit to his authority. We need to do marriage his way. We need to resist the siren song of political correctness. We need to constantly remember that marriage is for God. It is about another marriage, and that marriage is ultimate. We need to constantly *celebrate,* not deny, the differences between the sexes. God created our sexual differences, and therefore, they are good and beautiful. Last, we need to also celebrate, not criticize, the unique contribution of the Bible. It alone, of all the world's religions, teaches the ontological equality of men and women.

Chapter 2 will extract four more principles about marriage from God's Genesis 2 paradise. They take us to the heart of the war between secular culture and the Bible.

STUDY QUESTIONS

- On a scale of 1-10 how close does your marriage approximate paradise? Why or why not?
- Are your expectations for marital happiness too low or too high? Explain.
- In what way does the doctrine of creation fortify us to resist the pressure of political correctness?
- Which of the purposes for marriage can you remember? Does it surprise you that God's glory is his ultimate purpose? Why or why not? How does this change how you relate to your spouse?
- The world denies the differences between the sexes, but God expects us to celebrate them. What can we do to celebrate the differences?
- What happens in Genesis 2 that stresses that equality of value between Adam and Eve?

TWO: A Politically Incorrect Paradise

GOD GRACIOUSLY REVEALED his plan for marriage in Genesis 2. In experience, it was paradise. The first chapter of this book began to describe it. This chapter will finish that description, but to do so we will need to offend political correctness. In fact, everyone that wants to have the marriage God intended will, at some point, need to be politically incorrect.

Political correctness is a social death wish. It is a form of social suicide. Think of it as rational people bludgeoned into believing an obvious lie. Think of it as propaganda. The Soviet dictator, Vladimir Lenin (1870-1924) was a master propagandist. He famously said that if you repeat a lie enough times people will eventually believe it. That is how political correctness works. It deceives by repeating a thousand small lies. Its mouthpieces are the media, our educational institutions, and the coercive power of the state. They preach a lie until we finally believe something that we all once universally assumed to be untrue.

For example, Dr. Leonard Sax, is an M.I.T. graduate who speaks extensively to educators about the differences between boys and girls. In his important book, *Why Gender Matters,* he wrote, "Not only do most of the books currently in print about girls and boys fail to state the basic facts about innate differences between the sexes, many of them promote a bizarre form of *political correctness*, suggesting that it is somehow chauvinistic even to hint that any innate differences exist."[1] How can political correctness believe that men and women are the same physically, emotionally, socially, and mentally, when men and women are obviously and demonstrably different?

Genesis 1 and 2 contain some politically unpopular truths, and we must engage them if our marriages are going to return to paradise. The first is that, although men and women are equal in value, to produce different and complementary functions in marriage and parenting, God created men and women different. Second, he created marriage so that couples could share the joy of children. Third, he created marriage to be the union of a man and woman only. And fourth, he established marriage as the normative adult social status.

DIFFERENT IN FUNCTION

Nancy attended a prestigious all-girls school in California. Before her 1973 graduation she became a founding member of the campus' N.O.W. chapter. She left college completely convinced that the differences between boys and girls were not biological. They were socialized into children through their parent's expectations.

So, when Nancy had twins—Jeremy and Jennie—she and her husband expected their children to prove their thesis. When the children reached two, they bought dolls and trucks and placed them in the play room. Then for six months, expecting androgyny, they passively observed expecting Jeremy and Jennie to spend equal time with the trucks and dolls. They also assumed there would be no difference in *how* they played with them.

Surprise! Despite their parent's total passivity, Jeremy immediately gravitated to the trucks. He spent most of his time pushing them, and to their chagrin, occasionally aggressively running over the dolls. How about Jennie? She had little interest in trucks. Instead, she held, dressed, and cuddled the dolls. She wrapped them in blankets, laid them in the trucks, and then pretended to drive them to the hospital.

Nancy was more honest than many. She was willing to go where the evidence pointed. After this experience, and careful observation of how men and women *actually* relate, she rejected her politically correct college propaganda. She concluded that the biological differences between the sexes are obvious and should be to even the slowest observer.

Although Nancy was not a Christian, what she observed was God at work. God designed men and women differently. He created us to *complement* what each other lacked. He created us to find our greatest joy in serving each other differently. In the words of noted psychologist, Larry Crabb, "The sexes are distinct in what they are fundamentally designed to give and in what brings them the greatest joy in relationship... At the deepest level a man serves a woman differently than a woman serves a man."[2] Note: both sexes serve, but God has hard-wired into our natures the ability to get joy from loving and serving in a way unique to our biological sex.

In addition, to maximize his glory and our happiness, God created Adam and Eve in a relational "hierarchy." "Hierarchy" has become a negative word. We are sinners, and sinners use hierarchies to oppress their subordinates. However, when God created Adam and Eve there was no sin—just self-giving love.

MARRIAGE IN PARADISE

In this climate, there was no possibility of abuse. In God's kingdom, leaders exhaust themselves serving their followers. In God's kingdom leadership is not a privilege. It is a responsibility. It is a call to lavish service. To the degree that men lead this way, hierarchies liberate the women and children that take shelter under their leadership.

In God's paradise, everyone serves. To serve Eve, God gave Adam authority over her. Adam's job was to use his authority to further Eve's happiness, if necessary, at his expense. In the same way, God created Eve to serve and follow Adam. It was to be Adam's happiness at her expense. For both husband and wife, mutual servanthood is the way back to God's Paradise.

GOD SUBMITS

God's Son submitted to authority in the work of redemption, therefore we should not find submission to authority demeaning. He did this because headship and submission are aspects of God's glory. The Father and Son are ontologically equal. That means they are both fully God, equally divine, and each possessing life in themselves. Neither had a beginning. Neither will ever have an ending. Father and Son have always existed in perfect equality. Yet the Son made it his greatest joy to submit to his Father. "I *delight* to do your will, Oh my God! Your law is within my heart" (Psalm. 40:8).

It was a relationship of total dependence. "The Son can do nothing of his own accord, but only what he sees the Father doing. For whatever the Father does, that the Son does likewise" (John 5:19).

It was a relationship of total obedience. "I always do the things that are pleasing to him" (John 8:29).

If the Son of God "delighted" to submit to his equal, then submission must be a beautiful thing, an opportunity to share in God's life, a glorious privilege that expresses the very heart and soul of ultimate reality. And in fact, that is the case. The exercise of servant headship, and submission to it, is a first sign that God's kingdom has come in someone's life. Tragically, many Christians don't see it this way.

Years ago, I ran into resistance over kingdom hierarchy from a single woman named Martha.[3] Engaged in Christian ministry, she overheard a conversation about the Bible's teaching on a wife's duty to submit to her husband. "That's not fair," she objected. "Submission is demeaning. It's a form of gender-slavery. If men and women are equal, female subordination must be wrong. The word implies inferiority, and women are not inferior."

Because I was a new Christian I didn't know what to say. Thankfully, a more mature friend overheard the conversation and stepped in.

"Anyone who really feels that way doesn't understand God," he said. "Even though the Son of God is equal with God the Father, He delighted to submit to the Father's authority in the work of redemption, and for 2,000 years the church has held this position. If this is true, submission by a faithful wife to a loving husband is not demeaning. It is a sign of spiritual maturity."

Although my friend's attempts to persuade Martha did not work, I learned some key lessons. Those who know God know that being in authority does not imply superiority, nor does submission imply inferiority. God calls every Christian (male and female) to submit to lawful authority. Why? Because God himself values headship and submission.

This is why the New Testament devotes a surprisingly large number of verses to this subject. God commands wives to submit to husbands (Ephesians 5:22-34), children to parents (Eph 6:1-4), and slaves to masters (Ephesians 6:5-9). Colossians chapter three repeats these commands (3:18-4:1). The New Testament commands all believers to submit to their pastors (Hebrews 13:17), and all Christians to submit to civil authority (Romans 13:1-7, 1 Peter 2:13-3:7).

Submission is a significant New Testament subject, and in every case the "submitter" is ontologically equal to the person in authority. Never does the command to submit suggest or imply inferiority in the one supporting, submitting, or following. Therefore, if the problem is submission, we must throw out the entire New Testament. But, the problem isn't submission.

The problem is sin. We live in a fallen world. We are rebels. We don't like anyone telling us what to do. We want autonomy. We want complete freedom to do what we want, when we want, with whomever we want. In addition, we fear submission because sometimes authorities use their authority selfishly. Therefore, submission to authority is often fraught with pain. But here is a simple truth. If you don't like submission you won't like heaven, because heaven is a place where everyone joyfully and exuberantly submits to authority. In his book, *Knowing God,* theologian, J.I. Packer, sums it up this way.

> Thus, the obedience of the God–man to the Father while he was on earth was not a new relationship occasioned by the Incarnation, but the continuation in time of the eternal relationship between the Son and the Father in heaven. As in heaven, so on earth, the Son was utterly dependent upon the Father's will.[4]

TEAMWORK

God made Adam and Eve different to accomplish a task. The task was glorifying God by filling the earth with his image and likeness. That meant babies (Genesis 1:26-28). They were a team, and like any good team, to accomplish the assignment, to win the game, they needed to specialize and submit to a central authority.

Everyone who has played sports understands this. To be successful each athlete must use his skills and abilities to complement what his teammates lack. A basketball team might have both a six-foot-seven power forward and a five-foot-ten point guard. They win by exploiting each other's strengths and complementing each other's weaknesses. Their unity comes from submission to a common authority, the coach. If each player does his own thing, they will lose. If each player is five-feet-ten inches tall they will lose. The team that best maximizes each other's strengths, complements each other's weaknesses, and submits to the coach usually wins. The old expression says it all. There is no "I" in team.

In the same way, large corporations don't gain market share without specialization and submission to a common authority. Armies don't win battles without specialization and submission to common authority. If this is true in every area of life why are we so against it in marriage?

Complimenting each other's weaknesses is the way life works. It is the way God designed us to operate.

HELP NEEDED!

God created Eve to help Adam. She complemented him. She made up for what he lacked. The first time God said something negative about creation was Genesis 2:18. "It is not good that the man should be alone." Not good? Was Adam inadequate? Yes! To accomplish God's assignment, he needed someone who could do what he couldn't. "I will make him a *helper* fit for him" (Genesis 2:18b). The Hebrew word translated "helper," ezer, does not imply inferiority. The ESV Study Bible notes that this word refers to one "who supplies *strength* in the area that is lacking in 'the helped.' In fact, Psalm 121 uses the word to describe God himself (Psalm 121:1-2)."[5] He is our ultimate Helper.

MARRIAGE IN PARADISE

In other words, God created Eve to make up for Adam's inadequacies. He created her to love him, encourage him, support him, and yield to his leadership. God did not create Eve to be a "doormat." That is a perversion of God's intention. Rather, God created Eve—when appropriate— to "help" Adam with honest critique.

Jonathan Edwards and his wife, Sarah, are a good model of what God intended. Many still consider Edwards (1703-58) North America's greatest theologian. Together, their first mission was the extension of God's kingdom through the success of Jonathan's calling. Their second mission was discipling and nurturing their eleven children. Without Sarah's partnership they would not have been able to accomplish these goals. Today, we enjoy the legacy of Edwards' academic work because of Sarah's selfless service. In that sense his accomplishments are theirs together.

Sarah was an amazing woman. She was a highly accomplished, organized, and capable household administrator. She homeschooled their numerous children, managed their livestock (cattle, pigs, chickens), paid the bills, supervised the household servants, cared for their garden, and fed and housed the various theological students who sat under Jonathan's tutelage. And, because there were no hotels in 18th century Northampton, Massachusetts, the Edwards' home boarded, fed, and entertained any dignitaries passing through.

Sarah married Jonathan to help him accomplish God's call on his life. They were a team. When he wasn't traveling, Jonathan spent twelve hours a day in his study preparing sermons, answering correspondence, reading, and writing his important theological dissertations. He also tutored the interns that studied under him. None of this would have been possible without Sarah. Jonathan and Sarah's marriage pictures what Christian marriage is supposed to look like—mutual dependency and diversification of function. Sarah and

Jonathan understood that he was the leader and that it was her job to submit to him and respect him.

However, like every happy marriage, theirs was not primarily about headship and submission. It was about mission. It was about affection. They were a team. They were single-mindedly committed to the goal that God had called them to accomplish *together*. Outsiders described their union with words like love, affection, romance, and tenderness. But, mutual assent to God's hierarchy was the external framework that held it all together.

SERVANT LEADERSHIP

Adam had a different role. At a minimum, he had three responsibilities.

- Serving Eve by Leading her
- Serving Eve by Providing for her
- Serving Eve by Protecting her

First, God created Adam to lead. God made that obvious by creating him before Eve.

God also made Adam's leadership role obvious when he commanded him not to eat from the Tree of the Knowledge of Good and Evil *before* he created Eve. This means that Adam was responsible to explain God's command to Eve. In the words of Ephesians five he was to "wash her with the water of God's word."

Last, God made his leadership role obvious by holding Adam, not Eve, responsible for their marriage. Although Eve was the first to eat from the forbidden Tree, scripture never calls it the sin of Eve. It is always the sin of Adam. That is because Adam, as the servant leader, was responsible to God for both himself and Eve. This is why God came to Adam, not Eve, after their disobedience.

> But the LORD God called to the man and said to him, 'Where are you?' And he said, 'I heard the sound of you in the garden, and I was afraid, because I was naked, and I hid myself' (Gen. 3:9-10).

Second, not only was Adam to serve by leading, but he was to serve by providing. God commanded Adam to "work and keep" the garden (Gen. 2:15). This means that he was the provider. God did not create Eve to provide. He created Eve to help Adam provide (Vs. 18).

Third, due to his larger size, more aggressive disposition (a function of testosterone), and fifty percent greater upper body strength,[6] it was obvious that God created Adam to be the protector.

By themselves a group of sopranos is not that interesting. But complement them with alto, tenor, and bass and you have harmony. In the same way, harmony, or symphony, was God's intention with Adam and Eve. It is still God's intention, but it will only happen if we honor and celebrate the differences between men and women.

God created Adam and Eve equal in value but different in function. He also created them to conceive and parent children, and this is the second aspect of God's paradise that is politically incorrect.

THE JOY OF CHILDREN

Second, not only did God create men and women different, but he also created us to have children. But, to many couples children are a problem, and that is increasingly the perspective of Western culture. "Our day-to-day experiences" notes well respected demographer, Phillip Longman, "and the impressions we gather from the media, repeatedly suggest that population growth threatens whatever quality of life we enjoy...We can only shake our heads when we read that world population continues to increase by 75 million every year."[7]

Longman describes the way many have been trained to think and feel about children. For many, children are now the number one threat to our future. But falling fertility rates, not too many children, are our real problem. They are falling because marriage, children, and procreation are increasingly unpopular. World populations are shrinking. If current trends continue Japan, Russia, Italy, Germany, France, Australia, Eastern Europe, etc. will all face the dark specter of massive depopulation.

In addition, anxiety about overpopulation flies in the face of God's command. "God blessed them. And God said to them, 'Be fruitful and multiply and fill the earth'" (Genesis 1:28). Children are not a problem. They are a "blessing." Raised in the discipline and instruction of the Lord, children are a source of joy, happiness, and fulfillment. [8]

To "multiply and fill the earth" means, where possible, more than two children. That is because we need a total fertility rate (TFR) of 2.1 children per female to keep the population from falling. If each woman has just one child, the population will decrease rapidly. So, two children are not "multiplication." More than two are needed.

Paul Ehrlich's book, *The Population Bomb* (published in 1968), has made celebrating children counterintuitive. His book sold six million copies and predicted that, due to exploding world population, a billion would starve by 1983. Ehrlich, a professor at Stanford, was anti-natal. He was also instrumental in kick-starting the environmental movement.

But Ehrlich's predictions did not happen. Billions did not starve. Instead, the "green revolution" multiplied world food supplies faster than world population grew. In 2017, almost fifty years later, we have more calories per capita than at any time in history. Nevertheless, the fear of runaway population growth still haunts our collective conscience.[9] Ehrlich's ideas have been instrumental in shaping our collective attitudes towards fertility.

Secularism also reduces our desire for children. Longman notes that the number one cause of falling fertility is secularism, the worldview that discounts the spiritual dimension.[10] Secularism devalues family and relationships. To the secular mind all that matters is the material—what we can detect with our five senses. Secularism provides no basis for altruism. Instead, it promotes selfishness, and selfish people are reluctant to have children. That is another reason why secularism diminishes fertility rates.[11]

Gender feminism has also contributed to the falling TFR. Equity feminism was the 1960s movement that gave women equal political and social rights—rights that Christians support. However, in the 1970s equity feminism morphed into gender feminism. Ambitious to be like men, gender feminists denied the physical, mental, emotional, and social differences between the sexes.

The motor that drives gender feminism is an ugly selfish ambition. The key word is "selfish" not "ambition." Selfish ambition is my success *at the expense* of those around me, i.e. my husband or children. Influenced by selfish ambition, children became a problem, an obstacle to female ambition. It is hard to be an attentive mother and climb the career ladder at the same time. Something must give.

Gender feminism rules the academic world. That is why there is a direct relationship between the amount of education a woman has and her willingness to marry or reproduce. "The best predictor of fertility," notes Longman, "is the education of the female. In general, the more education a woman enjoys the fewer children she will have…Non-Hispanic white women with college degrees will complete their childbearing with just 1.7 children on average."[12] This means our brightest women are not producing, and this portends a tremendous drain on our future social capital.

In an article in *Foreign Policy Magazine,* Longman notes one exception. Whenever married men practice loving, benevolent leadership in the home, fertility rates go up. In other words, male investment in both women and children liberates women to value nurturance and fertility.[13] When we celebrate the male-female differences couples are "fruitful" and they "multiply."

Christians are in favor of female education. We want our wives and daughters to be educated—the more the better. The problem is not education. The problem is the secularism and selfish ambition that often accompanies advanced education. Secularism, coupled with selfish ambition, is the assassin of fertility.

God loves children, and so should we. "Behold children are a heritage from the Lord, the fruit of the womb a reward. Like arrows in the hands of a warrior are the children of one's youth. *Blessed* is the man who fills his quiver with them" (Ps. 127:3-5). I have never talked to anyone over fifty who wished they'd had fewer children.

Marriage Is Heterosexual

Third, God created marriage to be between a man and a woman. God created Adam and Eve, not Adam and Steve. This means that homosexual marriage is an oxymoron. It is contrary to nature. It is outside of God's plan. It is a diabolical attack on God's plan for a male-female union reflecting his image and likeness. If current trends continue, the church may be the only venue where marriage is clearly confined to the union of one man and one woman.

Same sex marriage is also a form of marriage inflation. It dilutes the meaning of marriage. When the money supply grows too fast the dollar inflates. It has less buying power. In the same way, redefining marriage to mean more and more devalues it, making it less meaningful, causing it to lose its inherent dignity and attractiveness.

Because the arguments used to normalize homosexual union can also be used to normalize polygamy, polyandry, incest, bestiality, etc., we can logically expect the normalization of these perversions to follow. The horse is out of the barn, and who will bring it back?

To highlight the beauty of the gem, Jewelers show off their diamonds against a black velvet cloth. In the same way, God's plan for marriage will increasingly shine against the background of our current spiritual darkness. In that we rejoice. Even though the meaning and value of marriage is in free fall, God will use our perversions for his glory.

MARRIAGE IS NORMATIVE

Last, God created marriage to be normative. In the Bible, it is the normal adult state.

A teller at my local bank flashed a new diamond ring. When I expressed admiration, she told me that she had a ten-month-old son, and that she didn't want to be working.

"Why don't you quit? You have a husband? I'm sure he would be willing to support you."

"Oh, I am not married," she said. "It's just a promise ring."

"I'm sorry," I said with embarrassment. "I assumed you were married. Why are you putting it off?"

"It's too expensive," she responded. "We can't afford to buy a house and get married at the same time, so we bought the house. The house is our priority. Marriage can wait."

This young lady spoke for millions. She did not assume that marriage needed to come before pregnancy and childbirth, or that anyone would think her priorities shameful. Basically, marriage just wasn't very important. The assumption that marriage matters, that it is the normal rite of passage into adulthood, that it should precede parenthood, that it is somehow crucially important, has taken wings and flown away.

In 1960, approximately ten percent of American adults were single. In his 2012 book, *Coming Apart,* Charles Murray notes that, for the first time in history, over fifty percent of

America's adults are now single.[14] That astounding shift took place in only fifty short years. Marriage has become rare, and that will increasingly be a source of unspeakable sorrow.

Tragically, it is not that different in the church. My oldest daughter attended a large church in Seattle, Washington that contained several thousand singles between the ages of 25 and 40. The pastor repeatedly urged the men to find an eligible female, pursue her, and get married. (There was a plentiful supply). But, the men were slow to respond. A pastor from an evangelical church in downtown London recently shared with me that they have a similar problem.

Obviously, singleness is not a sin. There are good reasons to be single. To better serve the church, Jesus and Paul remained single. Some Christian workers today do the same. Others would like to be married, but through no fault of their own, have not been able to find a suitable mate. Some are widows or widowers. However, the creation narrative in Genesis 1 and 2 implies that God intends marriage to be the normal adult state. The command in Genesis 1:28 to "Be fruitful, multiply, and fill the earth" was not for the elite few. This only happens when people marry.

As we have noted, the first time God found anything wrong with creation was when he looked at Adam and said, "It is not good that the man should be alone" (Genesis 2:18). Gloria Steinem, one of the architects of gender-feminism, disagreed. She famously wrote that "a woman needs a man as much as a fish needs a bicycle." But God created most men and women with an empty space that only a spouse and children can fill. Gloria Steinem eventually agreed. At age 66 she married David Bale. Three years later he died of brain cancer. Reportedly, she was devastated with grief.

Maybe a fish needs a bicycle after all?

God is pleased when we marry in our youth, have children earlier rather than later, live to a ripe old age, and set such a winsome example of marital bliss that our children and grandchildren rush to imitate us.

MAXIMIZING JOY

Cheeseburgers In Paradise are nice, but marriage in paradise is better. Over every married couple seeking to glorify God are these powerful words. *"And God blessed them"* (Genesis 1:28). God blesses marriage. God blesses couples determined to do marriage his way.

God finished his work of creation with these words, "And God saw everything that he had made, and behold, it was very good" (Genesis 1:31). This included marriage. "Very good" meant peace with God and man. It meant joy, emotional wholeness, and the absence of stress. It meant the absence of selfish ambition. It meant relational wholeness. It meant the capacity and willingness to love sacrificially; in other words, God's blessing was about people loving one another with God's love. God's blessing meant unbroken happiness in the presence of God and one another. For this reason, the second chapter of Genesis ends on a high note.

> A man shall leave his father and mother and be joined to his wife and the two shall become one flesh. And the man and his wife were both naked and were not ashamed (Gen. 2:24-25).

"One flesh" meant relational unity, unity of purpose, and emotional oneness pursued by two people complementing each other with diverse abilities and skills. It meant two very different people united in such a profound way that their relationship has produced a third person, the marital community—the Joneses, the Smiths, or the Williamses. It makes two people better and more useful as a couple than either was single. The sum of two is more than two. It is two plus something more...

"Naked and not ashamed" is also important. It meant an absence of shame, inferiority, or insecurity. Adam and Eve were happy with each other. They were best friends. They loved each other. They had no secrets. They had nothing to hide. They did not look down on each other. They enjoyed guilt-free sex as God meant it to be enjoyed—in the context of a committed, life long, monogamous relationship of mutual serving and loving. Does it get any better than this? All of this happiness is a result of following God's script.

"There is no more lovely, friendly or charming relationship, communion or company, than a good marriage," observed Martin Luther. Even the ancient Greek philosopher, Socrates, said, "My advice to you is to get married: if you find a good wife you'll be happy; if not, you'll be a philosopher."

However, we all know that marriage in paradise is not the experience of many. Often the dance between the sexes is broken. Why? Adam and Eve rebelled in Genesis 3, and the first casualty was God's plan for marriage. We now live in a Genesis 3 world, a world under the effect of sin. The rebellion in Genesis 3, and its consequences for marriage, are the subject of the next chapter.

STUDY QUESTIONS
- How do the four principles from Genesis 2, highlighted in this chapter, conflict with modern ideas about marriage and marital roles?
- Are you willing to walk out these principles, be identified with them, and take the scorn and ridicule that will come? Why or why not?
- God gave Adam and Eve specific roles to fulfill in marriage. In what way do those roles point us to eternal realities inherent in the godhead? Expand on your answer.
- Who has the tougher God-assigned role, the husband or the wife? Support your answer.
- How should a husband or wife respond when their spouse is not seriously trying to walk out the role God has assigned them?

THREE: Paradise Lost

CHAPTERS ONE AND TWO discussed God's plan for marriage which he designed to be a paradise in experience. The Holy Spirit describes it in Genesis 1:26 through 2:25. The bottom line is simple: God is good. He loves his people. He designed men and women biologically, emotionally, and mentally to serve and complement each other. God created us equal in value but different in function. He did this to maximize both his glory and our happiness.

However, by the end of Genesis 3 Adam and Eve have rebelled against God's plan. Their rebellion produced a spiritual tsunami that turned God's paradise into a wilderness. It affected Adam and Eve, each person descended from them, and the entire cosmos entrusted to their care. This chapter describes how that tsunami has affected marriage.

It would be hard to exaggerate the consequences. Sin now separated our happy couple from God himself, the source of all human thriving. God "drove out the man, and at the east of the garden of Eden he placed the cherubim and a flaming sword that turned every way to guard the way to the tree of life" (Genesis 3:24).

Sin also changed their nature. Pride, unbelief, selfishness, irritability, and greed were now a daily experience. Not only did sin separate them from God, but it also conspired to separate them from each other.

Although the next chapter is about the gospel, God's rescue plan, you cannot appreciate the gospel remedy until you understand how sin has affected marriage. So, to illustrate, we begin with the story of a contemporary couple.[1]

SAM AND CATHY

Sam and Cathy have been married for ten years. They have a seven-year-old and son and daughters aged four and two. Neither were Christians when they got married. Through the testimony of a neighbor, Cathy converted, and became a member of First Church. After two years of admiring Cathy's zeal, and feeling great conviction, Sam also began attending church. Both now believe the gospel, have been baptized, and are growing in their faith. However, like most of us, their marriage does not reflect the paradise described in Genesis 1 and 2.

Their pastor regularly preaches about Christian marriage. Through his sermons, Sam has learned that God wants him to passionately love Cathy as Christ loved his church. He knows this means sacrifice. In addition, he knows it means a willingness to lead his family, especially in spiritual matters.

By contrast, Cathy has learned that, as the church submits to Christ, God wants her to submit to Sam's leadership. She has also learned that she is supposed to respect and encourage her husband. However, for both Sam and Cathy this is all new. Although they want to live this way, three pieces of past baggage make it difficult.

The first piece of baggage is their upbringing. Neither have ever seen Christian marriage modeled. In fact, they have witnessed the exact opposite. Sam's parents divorced when he was eight. Contact with his father was limited to vacations. He has never watched a man model servant leadership. Lacking a husband, his mother ran everything. In Sam's eyes, women are strong and men are weak. That has been his experience.

He graduated from Michigan State University with a master's degree in computer science and went to work for a technology start up in Silicon Valley.

Cathy grew up in a two-parent household. However, her dad was passive, and her mother was the omni-competent family leader. Emulating her mother, Cathy became an outstanding student athlete, eventually earning a soccer scholarship to Cal Berkeley. She graduated and went to work in human resources for one of Sam's Silicon Valley competitors. In their late twenties, they met at a party, started dating, and got married. Sam was 30 and Cathy was 29.

A second piece of baggage is cultural pressure. Sam and Cathy grew up in a world that highly valued female achievement. For example, Cathy's high school student body president was a female, the valedictorian was female, and eighteen of the top twenty-five GPAs in her class belonged to women. In college, everyone assumed that a full-time career was the appropriate ambition for an intelligent, talented woman. Marriage and children could wait. The immediate goal was career development, not family. Anything less was a capitulation to "patriarchal power structures."

Feminism also affected Sam. As we have seen, his mother led his family, and except for varsity sports, women also dominated his high school experience. Therefore, his masculine identity has become fragile. Working with other men attracted him, but that kind of work was almost non-existent. In academics, politics, and business, women were increasingly at the center, and he had learned to live with it. Sometimes he felt like a member of the "second sex." When he first heard the teaching that male leadership in home and church was God's plan he felt insecure and inadequate. He had no category for this approach to men and women's roles, and he didn't know how to respond.

The third piece of baggage was patterns of relating. Their first year of marriage was a power struggle. Who would lead? There were fights and discussions. Cathy was an energetic, dominant personality. This coupled with Sam's general insecurity about the place of men in home and society, ultimately decided the issue. Sam slowly abdicated. He retreated into sports, business, and hunting. Cathy was capable, and she liked responsibility. Besides the constant fighting just wasn't worth it. Nevertheless, Sam felt emasculated. In darker moments, he often resented the feelings of uselessness that plagued him.

In addition, Cathy sometimes resented Sam. Now that they were Christians, she wanted him to be a spiritual leader for their children. She wanted him to be more interested in spiritual things, to be a spiritual leader for her as well, one that she could look up to and respect. However, Sam did just the opposite. He increasingly withdrew.

Like so many, the combination of their upbringing, cultural pressure, and well-worn patterns of relating, combined to sabotage their attempts to walk out a biblical marriage.

Neither Sam nor Cathy were happy with the way they related to each other. They didn't know it, but they suffered from a problem that had its roots in the breakdown of Adam and Eve's relationship. The third chapter of Genesis explains it.

Paradise Lost

TEMPTATION

Genesis 3 opens with a new character—the Serpent, and he has one goal in mind, to morph the happy couple into his own diabolical image. So, with great subtlety he did everything in his power to turn God's plan upside down.

> Now the serpent was more crafty than any other beast of the field that the LORD God had made. He said to the woman, "Did God actually say, 'You shall not eat of any tree in the garden?'" And the woman said to the serpent, "We may eat of the fruit of the trees in the garden, but God said, 'You shall not eat of the fruit of the tree that is in the midst of the garden, neither shall you touch it, lest you die.'" But the serpent said to the woman, "You will not surely die. For God knows that when you eat of it your eyes will be opened, and you will be like God, knowing good and evil." So when the woman saw that the tree was good for food, and that it was a delight to the eyes, and that the tree was to be desired to make one wise, she took of its fruit and ate, and she also gave some to her husband who was with her, and he ate. Then the eyes of both were opened, and they knew that they were naked. And they sewed fig leaves together and made themselves loincloths (Genesis 3:1-7).

These seven verses contain tremendous lessons. Under temptation, the order that God established in Genesis 2 broke down.

Because the Serpent was "crafty" he bypassed Adam, the spiritual head, and engaged Eve directly. She complicated things when she didn't consult her husband but acted independently. Watching the entire conversation, Adam must have sensed trouble, nevertheless he failed to intervene. Eve took matters into her own hands, and Adam responded with passivity.

MARRIAGE IN PARADISE

We saw in chapter one and two how God created Adam and Eve in a relationship of governmental order. God created Adam to be the servant-leader—leading Eve by serving and serving Eve by leading. Also, God created Eve to yield to Adam's leadership, to help him, and to respect him. God created her to help Adam fulfill his God-given calling. Looking back on Genesis 2, Paul sums it up this way. "The head of every man is Christ, the head of a wife is her husband, and the head of Christ is God" (1 Corinthians 11:3).

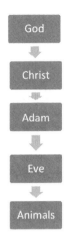

The Serpent had another agenda. He wanted God's place, at the top of the pyramid. He was crafty. He conquered by dividing. Bypassing Adam, he tempted Eve to rebel, then challenged Adam's authority through her. When Adam responded passively Eve became the functional head of their relationship.

Eve should have taken the Serpent's temptations to her husband. Instead, she entertained the Serpent's proposals independently. *I can handle this on my own*, she must have thought.

But Adam also failed. As we have seen, he overheard the entire conversation. He could have intervened. He should have sent the Serpent packing. Instead, he abdicated. When Eve brought him the forbidden fruit, he didn't say, "Eve, you know God's commandment. This is forbidden." Instead, scripture says, "She also gave some to her husband *who was with her, and he ate*" (3:6).

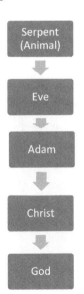

Why did Adam eat? We don't know for sure. Did he fear Eve more than he feared God? They had lived together in a sinless environment. Their relationship must have been electric. In God's immediate presence their relationship would have been richly fulfilling. So, when confronted with the temptation to please Eve or please God, did Adam chose the former? Did Adam love the gift (Eve) more than the Giver, God? The result was the inversion of God's order. An animal, (the Serpent), whom God created Adam to subjugate, had now taken God's place. The Serpent had inverted the beautiful order that God implemented in Genesis 2. It was now upside down.

The rest is history!

JUDGMENT

God's judgment was swift and specific. Although the sin came through Eve, as we have already observed, God held Adam responsible. "The Lord called to *the man* and said, 'where are you?'" (Gen. 3:9). Morphed and changed by indwelling sin, Adam and Eve immediately passed the buck. Adam blamed Eve and Eve blamed the Serpent (Vs. 12-13). Realizing what had happened, God pronounced judgment. He cursed the Serpent and judged the once happy couple's respective vocations.

Most importantly for this study, God judged the *relationship* between the man and his wife. The relationship that God created to be a paradise had now become a wilderness in experience. To Eve he said, "Your desire shall be for your husband, and he shall rule over you" (Gen. 3:16).

These words are important. In effect, God was saying, "You changed the good and holy order that I created you to experience. I meant for you to live in a relational paradise, but now you will experience discontentment with each other. Selfish ambition will pit you against each other. Eve will seek to control and dominate Adam, but he will respond with oppression, or at best passivity." Here is how the *ESV Study Bible* sums up Genesis 3:16.

> These words from the Lord indicate that there will be an ongoing struggle between the woman and the man for leadership in the marriage relationship. The leadership role of the husband and the complementary relationship between husband and wife that were ordained by God before the fall have now been deeply damaged and distorted by sin. This especially takes the form of inordinate desire (on the part of the wife) and domineering rule (on the part of the husband) ...the ongoing result of Adam and Eve's original sin of rebellion against God will have disastrous consequences for their relationship: (1) Eve will have the sinful "desire" to oppose Adam and to assert leadership over him, reversing God's plan for Adam's leadership in marriage. But (2) Adam will also abandon his God-given, pre-fall role of leading, guarding, and caring for his wife, replacing this with his own sinful, distorted desire to "rule" over Eve. Thus, one of the most tragic results of Adam and Eve's rebellion against God is an ongoing, damaging conflict between husband and wife in marriage, driven by the sinful behavior of both in rebellion against their respective God-given roles and responsibilities in marriage.[2]

Adam's sin meant the disintegration of God's script for marriage and family. Nevertheless, because God is merciful and gracious, all happiness did not disappear. Despite Genesis 3 couples continued to marry, and many still experienced significant happiness, but the total and complete happiness that God originally intended was gone.

Immediately after the third chapter of Genesis men began to oppress and use women. A dark veil descended over humankind. It corrupted God's image in the man and the woman. Think of the millions of rape and abuse victims around the globe. Think also about the thousands of angry women recently marching through Washington D.C. with pink "vagina hats" on their heads.

A new pattern emerged. Either men used women or ignored them. Likewise, women increasingly manipulated and used their husbands. Either way, for both husband and wife, it became my happiness at your expense. Marriage became a battle ground.

Men began to view women as sex objects. "And Lamech took two wives" (Gen. 4:19). For the same reason, Jacob took two wives *and* two concubines who constantly bickered.

Men and women used each other. Abraham turned Sarah into a shield to protect himself from Pharaoh (Gen 12), then Sarah manipulated Abraham into sleeping with Hagar. Through her son, Jacob, Rebecca manipulates her husband, Isaac (Genesis 27). Isaac used his wife, Rebecca, to protect himself from Abimelech (Genesis 26).

Sexual perversion also occurred. Genesis 19 introduces Sodom and Gomorrah and same-sex relations. Then Lot's daughters seduce their father (Genesis 19) and conceive Moab and Amon. Jacob's son, Judah, propositioned a temple prostitute, but got seduced by his daughter-in-law instead (Genesis 38).

And these are the Patriarchs—the men through whom God promised to bless planet earth.

"Your desire shall be for your husband, but he shall rule over you" became the new norm in human experience. We can lay the abuses of feminism, the sins of either passive or abusive men, dominant controlling wives, and weak, door mat wives all at the feet of Genesis 3:16.

Sin brought other pathologies into marriage as well—most notably, pride. Pride motivates us to use our spouse in selfish self-centered ways. It causes us to look down on our mates. It is also responsible for much of our insecurity and self-hatred.

Idolatry also became a major source of conflict. Idolatry is the tendency to worship someone or something other than God. It tempts us to make marriage and family ultimate, to expect from marriage what only God can give. This sin always ruins marriage and family life. We will examine each of these in subsequent chapters.

In summary, after Adam's sin a dark veil descended over the relationships between men and women. At no time in history has it been more pronounced. Today Western culture increasingly sees men as the oppressors and women as the oppressed. The abuses of men and the excesses of feminism have created an environment increasingly toxic to male-female relations. Hostility and suspicion are becoming the norm.

BACK TO SAM AND CATHY

All unredeemed couples experience at least some of God's Genesis 3:16 judgment. Some suffer more than others. As we have noted, because God is gracious many experience substantial happiness. But, although many Christian and non-Christian marriages are happy, none experience the relational paradise that God originally intended.

When our marriage makes us miserable, when the best mood descriptors are black or grey, when we feel restless, lustful, angry, bitter, jealous, selfish, or bored, we can trace it all back to Genesis 3.

The Serpent's tactics have not changed. He still attacks the family through wives. He still encourages them to act independently. He still motivates male passivity. He hates it when men become servant leaders and shoulder responsibility for their families. He hates it when men fear God's disapproval more than their wives. He hates it when women respect their husbands, trust God to work through their husband's leadership, and seek to serve and honor him.

Indwelling sin, a curse inherited from Adam and hard-wired into us from birth, explains Sam and Cathy's troubles. Sam's father divorced his mother. Cathy's father passively relinquished the reigns of authority to her mother. Sam and

Cathy are now trying to crawl out from under the wreckage of their parent's examples. In addition, their own sinful natures, inherited from Adam, have complicated the issue. Sam likes passivity. He has enough responsibility at work. One part of him hates the feeling that he is just a family appendage, but another likes the freedom from responsibility.

On the other hand, Cathy likes control. One part of her wants Sam to lead, another fears loss of control if he does.

There is a spiritual solution to their dilemma. It is the gospel, the first step back to paradise. The gospel increasingly frees us from the pain of Genesis 3. It is the doorway back into paradise, and God has kicked it wide open. Faith in Jesus' life, death, and resurrection forgives our sins, and unites us with Christ in fellowship. God's Holy Spirit motivates us to live a countercultural way of life. The gospel motivates husbands to become the servant leaders God initially intended. The gospel motivates wives to increasingly encourage that leadership and follow it. The result is a gradual increase in the love and fellowship that God created us to experience in paradise.

The journey is not easy, and it will never be fully completed in this life. However, the reward is more than worth the effort. How to get there is the subject of the next chapter.

STUDY QUESTIONS

- Does the story of Sam and Cathy remind you of anyone? Why?
- When Adam and Eve sinned, two judgments occurred. Which can you remember, and how does it affect marriage today?
- Why did the Devil tempt Eve instead of Adam? What does this tell us about the nature of temptation?
- How did the Serpent completely overturn God's plan for spiritual order in marriage? What does this say about the source of gender confusion in the contemporary West?
- How does God want you to respond to this chapter?

FOUR: Paradise Restored

I WANT TO OPEN THIS chapter with an important question. What makes a marriage Christian? It can't be love. Love is common to all marriages—whether Mormon, Muslim, secular, or Jewish. It can't be children. Men and women from all faiths marry to have children. It can't be communication techniques, skill in handling family finances, abhorrence of divorce, or even a successful sexual relationship. All marriages, Christian or not, pursue these.

I remember listening to a series of lectures on marriage by a Seattle pastor. What he said was excellent. He covered sex, communication, the handling of finances, and relating to in-laws. But I finished frustrated. Why? Any Jewish, Mormon, secular, or Muslim couple would have agreed. He failed to discuss the one element that makes a marriage specifically "Christian," a subject that would anger Jews or Mormons.

MARRIAGE IN PARADISE

So, back to our question. What makes a marriage specifically Christian? A Christian marriage seeks to model and glorify the relationship between Christ and his church created by the gospel. That is its primary purpose. We alluded to this in chapter one. Ephesians 5:22-33 explicitly states that purpose.

> Wives, submit to your own husbands, as to the Lord. For the husband is the head of the wife even as Christ is the head of the church, his body, and is himself its Savior. Now as the church submits to Christ, so also wives should submit in everything to their husbands. Husbands, love your wives, as Christ loved the church and gave himself up for her, that he might sanctify her, having cleansed her by the washing of water with the word, so that he might present the church to himself in splendor, without spot or wrinkle or any such thing, that she might be holy and without blemish. In the same way husbands should love their wives as their own bodies. He who loves his wife loves himself. For no one ever hated his own flesh, but nourishes and cherishes it, just as Christ does the church, because we are members of his body. 'Therefore, a man shall leave his father and mother and hold fast to his wife, and the two shall become one flesh.' *This mystery is profound, and I am saying that it refers to Christ and the church.* However, let each one of you love his wife as himself, and let the wife see that she respects her husband (Ephesians 5:22–33 italics mine).

Verse 32 soars to thirty-thousand feet, and from that perspective Paul states God's overarching purpose. "This mystery is profound, and I am saying that *it refers to Christ and his church.*" Here is Paul's point: God created the original union of Adam and Eve (and all subsequent marriages) to glorify, —i.e. display the beauty of—the marriage between Christ and his church. When Adam married Eve, she became his body. They became one flesh. In the same way, through the gospel, Christ marries his church and we become his body. We enter into a one-flesh union with him.

Christ is the head of his church. When a man and woman marry the same thing happens. The husband becomes the head of his wife, his body. Christ never divorces his church. In the same way, God designed marriage to be indissoluble. Because she is his body, how the husband treats his wife is how he treats himself.

These verses are Paul's attempt to restore marriage to its Genesis 2 paradise. He exalts the equality between the sexes while simultaneously upholding the different roles that God originally intended. In other words, Ephesians 5:32 refocuses marriage on its original goal—the glory of God. Paul's words take us back to the joy, the unity of purpose, and the oneness that God created Adam and Eve to enjoy.

Joyful submission to his servant love is the duty of Christ's bride. Because Christ loves his bride, submission is safe. It profits us. It is our happiness at his own expense', and that expense was *infinite*. Because Christ's leadership of the Church is tender and loving, the appropriate response is joyful submission.

Although the Holy Spirit has given us Ephesians five to take us back to Genesis 2, for many this ideal seems impossible. John and Kelsey are a good example.

CHANGE IS POSSIBLE

Opposite temperaments often attract, and this was the case with John and Kelsey. Kelsey was quiet, pensive, thoughtful, and cautious. She would rather give John control than go through conflict. John was outgoing, talkative, and energetic. His leadership style bordered on dictatorial. Temperamentally, they were opposites. Where John was dominating and controlling, Kelsey was passive and non-confrontational.

Four years after their marriage they both became Christians. When they began to understand God's order for marriage they became discouraged. John saw that God wanted him to lead, but with kindness, grace, and patience. God wanted him to free Kelsey to respond from her heart rather than his control. God wanted him to yield to Kelsey whenever possible, to make her happy, to seek her welfare, to honor her contribution with both words and action. It was his job to draw her out and listen carefully. This was not natural for him. He knew he needed to change, but it didn't seem possible.

On the other hand, God wanted Kelsey to give the reins of leadership and control to her husband. God wanted her to trust him to work through John, but God also wanted her to be more assertive. She was learning that doormat passivity did not please God, that John needed her input, and that to give it she would need to risk conflict. She was fearful. Could she trust God? Could she change and be more assertive?

Because both believed the gospel, change was possible. Because they believed God's word, they believed his plan was better than theirs. So, they applied themselves to Paul's instructions in Ephesians five. There were struggles. There were misunderstandings. There were growing pains. There was conflict. Both had to change, but both were willing. Faith that God's way of doing things was better than theirs motivated them.

Several decades later their temperaments have not changed. (That is because temperament is God's gift). Kelsey has learned to respect and defer to her husband's leadership, but in a more assertive way, one that pleases God. John has learned to take the initiative for family prayer and Bible study, communication, and servant love. He no longer seeks to force his wife's submission through dominance and control. Instead, he gently leads, confident in his calling, resting in God's equipping grace. Biblically speaking, theirs has become a model marriage. Now their adult sons and daughters imitate their parents. John and Kelsey are passing a wonderful legacy to future generations.

This story is important. Many reading it are like John and Kelsey, and they need hope.

LOVE BY RELATIONSHIP

Genesis 2 described the creation of Adam and Eve. It was a relationship of governmental order, undergirded by love and unselfishness. But, as we learned in chapter 3, when sin entered, Eve's "desire" became "for her husband." This meant she wanted to control and manipulate—to usurp his authority. Adam responded with either passivity or oppression. For the descendants of both Adam and Eve, the gospel is the antidote.

Love is a verb. "By this we know love that he *laid down his life for us,* and we ought to lay down our lives for the brothers" (1 Jn 3:16). This means that God's love is about *acting* not feeling. Yes, love usually produces the fruit of affection, but it doesn't require it. We've already noted the parallel definition— "your happiness at my expense." Either way, because action is foundational to God's love it should be foundational to marital love as well. "A new commandment I give to you, that you love one another" (Jn. 13:34). Because the marital covenant is the glue that holds civilization together, marriage is the most important relationship to see love worked out.

It's also important to note that how love expresses itself varies according to the relationship. So, for example, children love their parents differently than their classmates. Employees love their employers differently than their fellow employees. Christians love the local church by tithing, submitting to pastoral authority, and joining the church in its mission, but that is not how they love their employer. In the same way, how marital love expresses itself is specific to that relationship.

WIFE'S LOVE

For wives, love means submission to her husband's authority (Ephesians 5:22-24). It means respecting her husband's office. It means encouraging his leadership (Ephesians 5:22-24, 33). There is no way to sugarcoat or minimize this. But as we have noted, it does not mean the opposite—passivity or doormat-ishness. Submission means honest and forthright disagreement when necessary. The bold, competent, assertive woman described in Proverbs 31:10-31 is the best example. Biblical submission requires the resources of femininity's God-given strengths.

As we have seen, in contemporary culture submission is a dirty word. Few are willing to utter it, let alone teach on it. So, we have marriage conferences called Love and Respect. Respect is important, but it is not submission. In Ephesians five "respect" is secondary, but submission is the main idea.

We need a working definition of what obedience to Ephesians 5:22-24 looks like. In the real world, what does submission look like? The context is important. It is not the submission of a slave to a master. It is love. It is the most intimate tender, supportive relationship most people will ever experience. It is submission to a best friend, a romantic partner with whom she shares great affection. It is submission to an equal with whom she sleeps, shares her deepest thoughts, etc. There is no closer bond. They are lovers who deeply esteem each other. These realities shape her submission. John Piper sees submission as a toolbox of attitudes.

> The basic meaning of submission would be: recognize and honor the greater responsibility of your husband to supply your protection and sustenance; be disposed to yield to his authority in Christ, and be inclined to follow his leadership.[1]

New Testament theologian, Andreas Kostenberger, describes it as a disposition to follow.

> A more accurate way of looking at marital roles is to understand that wives are called to *follow their husband's loving leadership* in their marriage.[2]

And pastor and author, Ray Ortlund, helps us with a description of the opposite.

> The opposite...is an unsatisfiable demandingness, a fault-finding resistance, a tiresome fretfulness: 'A continual dripping on a rainy day and a quarrelsome wife are alike' (Prov. 27: 15). No man gets married in order to live under the leaky roof, so to speak, of a nagging, scolding wife.[3]

As we have already noted, the command to be submissive is not unique to wives. It applies to all Christians in various relationships.[4] It is the Christian duty to all in authority. How to walk it out is usually nuanced, but it is seldom easy.

Most importantly, as we have seen, Christ's submission to his Father is the model (Philippians 2:5-8). He was equal to his Father, yet he submitted. In addition, despite being vastly superior to every human authority, he humbled himself and submitted. Think of it! He submitted to the sinful, fallen creatures that he created—his parents, his Rabbi, and even Pontius Pilate. But because submission is the heart and soul of godliness, it was also his delight. In the same way, submission to authority is a mark of godliness for both men and women. It expresses great faith. For both sexes submission to authority is central to biblical piety.

FOUR LIMITATIONS

I want to make some qualifying statements about submission. First, a wife's duty to submit is not a license for her husband to demand his way. Infrequently, in a godly marriage, after weighing all the facts, and carefully listening to his wife's objection, a husband will make a decision with which she does not agree. Although most decisions in most Christian marriages are made by talking it over together, in a biblical marriage there is a clear understanding that when deadlocked, and a decision needs to be made, the husband has the tie breaking vote. However, a husband led by the Holy Spirit will use that vote cautiously and unselfishly.

Second, Ephesians five tells wives to, "submit to your own husbands." This means a woman's submission is not to men in general but only to her husband. Unlike Islam, Christian women do not submit to all men.

Third, Ephesians five says her submission is to be "as to the Lord." These four words are very important. They go to the heart of motivation. A godly wife submits to her husband not because she wants to please him, or because he is smarter, (he probably isn't), but because she wants to please the Lord. Ultimately, her submission is "to the Lord" not her husband. She submits to Christ who is not sinful, fallible, or fallen. He is perfect, and he promises to care for every woman that trusts him enough to risk submission to an imperfect husband.

Fourth, it is important to note that submission is never absolute. Should he ask her to do anything contrary to God's word, she is duty bound to say "no." "To be subject to her husband" notes Dr. Martyn Lloyd-Jones, "does not mean that she is the slave of her husband."[5] A wife's duty to be submissive never licenses her husband to ask her to do something contrary to conscience or not in line with God's will.

Last, the submission in Ephesians five produces unity of purpose. A godly Christian wife renounces the selfish ambition that is the hallmark of gender-feminism. She is ambitious, but it is not selfish. Like Christ, her ambition is other focused. It is for her husband and children's success. She has married her husband to help him fulfill God's calling. She has become the "helpmate" that God envisioned when he created Eve. They are a team. She might have a job outside the home, she might enjoy her job, she might be really good at her job, and she might glorify God through her job, but she never forgets her role of wife and mother. She and her husband have become one flesh, and they have one purpose together—the glory of God through the fulfillment of her husband's calling and the raising of godly offspring.

Summing up, Andreas Kostenberger writes, "While some may view submitting to one's husband's authority as something negative, a more accurate way of looking at marital roles is to understand that wives are called to *follow their husband's loving leadership* in their marriage."[6]

As we have already noted, every woman attempting to obey this text will need to swim against the current of cultural pressure. She must be willing to be misunderstood. She will need great courage. She will need to resist the ugly, sinful, rebellion that flavors Western culture's approach to everything biblical.

Husband's Role

However, the main idea in Ephesians five is not wifely submission: it is the husband's love. Just as Christ's love is the engine that shapes and motivates the church, so each husband's sacrificial love is the engine that shapes and energizes the Christian family. To emphasize this Paul devotes three verses to the wife's duties, *but six* to the husband's.

> Husbands, love your wives, as Christ loved the church and gave himself up for her, that he might sanctify her, having cleansed her by the washing of water with the word, so that he might present the church to himself in splendor, without spot or wrinkle or any such thing, that she might be holy and without blemish. In the same way husbands should love their wives as their own bodies. He who loves his wife loves himself. For no one ever hated his own flesh, but nourishes and cherishes it, just as Christ does the church, because we are members of his body (Ephesians 5:25–30).

What woman wouldn't gladly submit to a man who loved her as Christ loves his church? As we have seen, Christ's love is more than affection. It is his bride's happiness at his expense. It is about action. It has no thought for itself, but only for his bride. Every decision Christ makes is for our good, no matter the cost to himself. Christ's great love makes submission safe. In the same way, submission to a husband who is attempting to love his wife this way, is also safe.

However, every husband attempting to return to paradise differs from Christ in one crucial way: he is fallen. He has the capacity for great selfishness.

For example, my wife, Judy, has eye allergies. We normally sleep with the bedroom window open. After awaking several mornings with dry, irritated eyes, Judy became convinced that air-born allergens were the culprit.

"Bill, would you close our bedroom window tonight?"

It was hot and stuffy in the room, so I answered, "It's too hot."

Because she has a servant's heart, Judy went to sleep without complaining.

In the middle of the night I awoke under great conviction. "Husbands, love your wives as Christ loves his church." I got up, closed the window, and went back to sleep.

You might say, it was a small thing? Yes. It was a small thing, but here is where true love makes its grand entrance—in the small things of life.

The simple conclusion is obvious. Like most husbands, I love imperfectly. I wrestle with selfishness and unbelief. My capacity to love will not be perfected until I see Christ face to face. We all struggle with indwelling sin. However, there is an enormous difference between a man *trying* with all of his heart to return to paradise and a husband who is apathetic about his duty to love.

True love shows up in all the small details, like opening or closing windows. It is not passive. It actively and joyfully assumes responsibility. It does not oppress. Rather, it liberates.

When faced with a choice between a new shotgun or a sofa, love buys his wife a sofa. If his wife resents the fact that he spends too much time on the golf green he makes adjustments.

When his wife pleads with him to not throw his dirty clothes on the floor he listens and responds. When his wife complains because he spends two of his three vacation weeks fishing with his buddies, he quits fishing, or greatly reduces the time invested in fishing. The examples are endless. The home of a man that loves this way has a special aroma. It is joy—the spiritual fruit that always follows love in Galatians 5:22.

In addition, verses 26-27 command him to wash his wife with the Word. He does this with her eternal welfare in mind. "Cleansing her...that she might be holy and blameless." A woman just told my wife that after 25 years of marriage, her believing husband has never once opened the Bible and read it with her. I fear that this is too common in the church. Reading the Bible with your wife is an important way to wash her with the Word.

The husband who makes this his practice is on his way back to Genesis 2. God commanded Adam to refrain from eating from the forbidden tree, and it was his responsibility to share this with Eve. The formula has not changed. Washing your wife with the Word is not your pastor's job. It is not your small group leader's job. It is not the job of the radio or podcast preacher. If you are a husband, it is your responsibility.

Washing your wife with the word does not mean a formal teaching session. Rather, it means the willingness to initiate Bible reading and discussion with your wife. Some men keep a log of texts that will speak to their spouse's needs. Others read through a book of the Bible with her a chapter at a time. The ways to do this are endless.

The apostle Peter adds two additional duties—honor her and understand her. "Husbands, live with your wives in an *understanding way, showing honor* to the woman as the weaker vessel, since they are heirs with you of the grace of life, so *that your prayers may not be hindered*" (1 Peter 3:7).

What does it mean to live with your wife in "an understanding way?" It means sensitivity to her femininity. She is a woman. Every cell in her body has two X chromosomes. She thinks differently, feels differently, and responds differently. While your hormones are flat, hers are like a roller-coaster. God wants you to recognize this and respond with compassion, not criticism.

Second, God commands you to honor her. This means regular, private and public acknowledgment of your gratitude for her differences, her gifts, and her contribution to your marriage and family.

An old friend of mine is a slow learner. After forty years of marriage, he lamented that he had spent the first thirty-five trying to turn his wife into a man. He finally gave up and began to honor the beautiful way God created her differently.

God loves your wife intensely. He gave her to you as a gift. If you mistreat her there will be consequences. Peter warns that your "prayers will be hindered." That is because God responds to the prayers of those that listen to him. If this is a new idea to you, read Psalm 66:18, Isaiah 59:1-2, 65:12, 66:4, Zechariah 7:13, John 15:7, and 1 John 3:22. Peter's words are the marriage application of these verses. Unless you take seriously and sincerely God's commands to love your wife sacrificially, consider her needs, and honor her, God will not hear your prayers. When you pray to God for your children, that promotion you want, or the intimacy with God that you seek he might turn a deaf ear. Don't take this lightly. God hears the prayer of those who listen to him.

Paul gives each husband another serious motive for obedience. "He who loves his wife loves himself." You cannot selfishly use and abuse your wife and love yourself. Although sexual union makes us "one flesh," the happier, more contented, secure, and fulfilled your wife is, the happier you will become. As the old saying goes. "When momma ain't happy, nobody's happy."

Thinking of the husband's authority, Martyn Lloyd-Jones concludes, "We must remember that power is to be tempered by love. It is to be controlled by love, it is the power of love. No husband is entitled to say that he is the head of the wife unless he loves his wife."[7]

Don't Neglect this Teaching

Teaching about marriage is always more than Ephesians five, but it is never less. As we noted in the introduction, because of the offensiveness of this teaching, it is not unusual to hear teaching about marriage that neglects headship and submission.

However, when the Bible discusses marriage, it emphasizes structural authority. Since this is the biblical emphasis, it should be ours also. In fact, the New Testament epistles provide no instructions about how to live as husband and wife that are not in the context of headship and submission. Four times the New Testament letters discuss marriage. We have already discussed Ephesians five. Here are the other three. The italics are mine.

> But I want you to understand that the head of every man is Christ, the head of a wife is her husband, and the head of Christ is God (1 Corinthians 11:3).

> Wives, submit to your husbands, as is fitting in the Lord. Husbands, love your wives, and do not be harsh with them (Colossians 3:18–19).

> Likewise, wives, be subject to your own husbands, so that even if some do not obey the word, they may be won without a word by the conduct of their wives, when they see your respectful and pure conduct. Do not let your adorning be external—the braiding of hair and the putting on of gold jewelry, or the clothing you wear— but let your adorning be the hidden person of the heart with the imperishable beauty of a gentle and quiet spirit, which in God's sight is very precious. For this is how the holy women who hoped in God used to adorn themselves, by submitting to their own husbands, as Sarah obeyed Abraham, calling him lord. And you are her children, if you do good and do not fear anything that is frightening. Likewise, husbands, live with your wives in an understanding way, showing honor to the woman as the weaker vessel, since they are heirs with you of the grace of life, so that your prayers may not be hindered (1 Peter 3:1–7).

Taking our marriages back to paradise is only possible through the liberating power of the gospel. The deeper we dive into the gospel the greater our marital joy and happiness.

Back to Genesis

The last chapter opened with the story of Sam and Cathy. For Sam, a return to paradise meant repentance from passivity. No man enters marriage equipped to love as Christ loves his church. Either he is too passive or too overbearing. The passive return to paradise by assuming responsibility, the overbearing by letting go of control and criticism. In either case this requires faith. The man who really believes that Ephesians five is a return to Paradise will pursue God's plan for biblical masculinity.

For Cathy, this also meant change. Women who really believe that Ephesians five is a return to paradise will submit to their husband because they trust the Lord (not always their husband). Trust in God's goodness empowers them to surrender control. To the degree that her submission is to the Lord, not her husband, it becomes joyful. Cathy believed the gospel. She believed that "God exists, and that he rewards those that seek him" (Heb. 11:6). Behind this conviction was a deeper one—*God is infinitely good.* I can trust him!

The gospel, culminating in the cross and resurrection, is the greatest display of God's goodness in history. If God is so good that, to forgive you and me, he would send his Son to be tortured to death on a splintered cross, he will surely *reward those who seek him.* Because Sam and Cathy share a growing conviction that this is also true, they have applied themselves to the practice of biblical headship and submission. They do this in the expectation of a liberal reward, both in this life (a renewed marriage), and in the life to come.

CONSUMMATION

I want to close this chapter with a reminder that human marriage is only for this life. Death severs the marital covenant. We only vow to love and serve our spouse until "death do us part." Jesus reminds us that there will be no human marriage in the world to come (Matt. 22:23-33).

For this reason, Christians don't expect their marriage to provide what only God can give. They don't expect ultimate fulfillment from their earthly mates. In our happiest moments, there is always an empty spot. Only God can fill it.

That is because only Christ can provide ultimate relational satisfaction. In this way the small joy's we get from human marriage point us to a greater joy, the eternal marriage of the church to Christ.

> And I saw the holy city, new Jerusalem, coming down out of heaven from God, prepared as a bride adorned for her husband (Revelation 21:2)
>
> Come, I will show you the Bride, the wife of the Lamb.' And he carried me away in the Spirit to a great, high mountain, and

showed me the holy city Jerusalem coming down out of heaven from God... (Revelation 21:9–11)

CONCLUSION

The attempt to glorify the union between Christ and his church is what makes a marriage Christian. It is about more, but never less than, biblical order. Husbands and wives love each other differently than they love others. God's marching orders are in Ephesians 5:22-33. They are the way back to paradise.

Gospel-focused couples find ample motivation to live this way. "Beholding the glory of the Lord we are transformed into his image from one degree of glory to another" (2 Corinthians 3:18).

Our relationship with Christ established through the gospel shows us what perfect headship and submission look like. Christ's marriage to his church is our model.

> And the angel said to me, 'Write this: Blessed are those who are invited to the marriage supper of the Lamb.' And he said to me, 'These are the true words of God (Revelation 19:9).

STUDY QUESTIONS

- What is the most important purpose of marriage? What makes a marriage Christian?
- God wants married couples to love each other two ways, structurally and personally. Define these and talk about which is most common to your marriage and why?
- Wives: what does a wife's submission look like? What does it mean, and what does it not mean? What limitations does God place on wifely submission?
- Husbands: what does it look like when a husband loves his wife as Christ loved his church?
- Why, when the Bible discusses marriage, does it emphasize structural love?
- What part does this chapter play in taking marriage back to Genesis 2?

FIVE: The Gospel

A FRIEND WHO TRAVELS and speaks at churches around the country, was recently asked his opinion about the spiritual health of the church. "There is a lot of gospel ignorance," he answered. "In some cases, it is amnesia. But whether they never knew it, or have long forgotten it, the current lack of gospel-clarity is a matter of great concern."

Understanding the gospel matters. We are not saved because we go to church or know the pastor. We are not saved by listening to sermons or having Christian parents. We are not saved because we raised our hand or went forward at a crusade, and we are not saved because our friends are Christians. We are only saved because we understand and *believe* the gospel and live a life increasingly consistent with that profession. That is why gospel-clarity is so important.

Before our church admits someone to membership we conduct a membership interview. The purpose is to ensure the applicant understands and believes the gospel. In addition, we only schedule an interview after someone has attended our new member's class, during which we explain the gospel in great detail.

To diagnose their gospel-clarity we ask open ended questions. For example, "If a friend asked what they must do to become a Christian what would you say?" Or, "If you were to die in your sleep tonight, and Christ were to ask you, 'Why should I let you into heaven?' what would you say?" Or, "In your own words, explain the gospel."

Even though many have been Christians for years, and they have heard a detailed explanation of the gospel at our new member's class, I am often surprised at the responses. One fiftyish male, who had been an elder in a large evangelical Church in the Southwest responded, "The gospel is the good news that Jesus died for my sins."

"Catholics also believe that, but there was a Reformation because they rejected the gospel. So, what do you need to add to that definition to make it evangelical?"

"You need to lead a good life," he answered. "I know I am not perfect, but I am at least as good as average." (If you are wondering, *What's wrong with that answer?* Keep reading).

Another man, who had also been an elder in two different conservative Presbyterian denominations, answered, "The gospel is the Ten Commandments."

I have listened to people working on graduate degrees in theology that couldn't explain the gospel. The most common bad answer goes something like this. "Just believe. God loves everyone. I figure if I am kind and forgiving to those around me, it will all work out."

We seldom get a straight forward, clear answer to the question, "What is the gospel?"

For this reason, no matter how long they have attended church, or been in Christian ministry, no matter how many theological degrees they have, we never assume that they understand, and can articulate, the gospel.

THEOLOGY PRECEDES PRACTICE

You might be asking, "What does the gospel have to do with marriage?" The answer is, everything! The concept that has the greatest influence over the spiritual joy in your marriage is your ability to understand and *apply* the gospel. That is because orthodoxy (the gospel) always precedes orthopraxy (application). I have written this chapter to help you and your spouse make that connection.

What you really believe, not what you say you believe, will ultimately shape your behavior. Shortly after my conversion, I attended a seeker sensitive church. Most of the sermons were about how to live the Christian life. They covered subjects like productivity, time management, marriage, parenting, how to build friendships, how to evangelize, how to forgive, etc. The preaching was rarely theological, and it always *assumed* the gospel. It rarely articulated the gospel, nor did it mine its deeper truths. Because, by God's grace, I was a student of the Bible, I had many theological questions, and the answers to those questions eventually drove me to change churches.

Although the decades have passed, I am still in contact with many of my old friends from that church, and the fruit has been discouraging. Some have quit going to church. A sizeable number are divorced and remarried. A large percent of the grown children have walked away from the faith. These are the fruits of marriage and family life divorced from gospel centrality.

A healthy church stresses theology—who God is, who we are, and what God has done for us. The result is real lasting transformation of marriage, parenting, and daily life. A friend, Mark, summed it up this way, "At the seeker-sensitive church, we knew *what* to do, but we didn't know *why* to do it. Now we know *why* to obey, and everything has changed."

The rest of this chapter is about the "why." The gospel does at least four things. It tells us *why* we should love our spouse. It shows us *what* that love should look like. It *motivates* us to love them, and it *lavishes us with grace and forgiveness* when we fail.

The gospel starts with the bad news. Without the bad news, the gospel (the good news) makes no sense.

THE BAD NEWS

The word "gospel" is a translation of a Greek word which means "good news." The gospel is a declaration of amnesty from our Heavenly King. We are at war with God, and through the gospel, God has moved to end the hostility. He wants peace. He wants to be our Father. He wants to adopt us, his enemies, into his family. This is good news.

However, the gospel is only *good* news to one who understands their problem. To everyone else, it is just news. If I offered one thousand dollars to a multi-millionaire he would probably thank me, but my offer would not be Good News. Why? He has more than enough money. What is a thousand dollars to him? But if I offered it to a homeless man living under a shopping cart in a rainstorm, he would probably leap, jump, and shout for joy. It would mean food, clothing, and a dry, warm place to sleep. That is how people respond who really understand their predicament—the bad news.

The bad news starts with God's holiness. God's children will spend eternity plumbing its depths and never reach the bottom. It is infinite. When the prophet, Isaiah, saw the Lord "high and lifted up," he also saw six-winged Seraphim hovering over his throne crying, "Holy, holy, holy is the Lord God Almighty. The whole earth is full of his glory" (Isaiah 6:3). They

The Gospel

are celebrating God's holiness, and watching them we learn some lessons.

First, God's holiness is infinite. The Cherubim repeatedly declare the glory of God's holiness. It is ongoing, and it is so deep and profound that they never tire or get bored of praising him for it.

Second, God's holiness is transcendent. Lest they irreverently gaze upon the perfections of his infinite holiness, they cover their eyes with two wings. With the other two they cover their feet for God's presence has even made the ground holy. With the remaining two they fly. Remember, these angels are sinless. They are not polluted with sin like you and me, and yet they still dare not stare directly at God in his holiness. No wonder the Bible repeatedly reminds us that no one can see God and live. The contrast between God's holiness and our sinfulness would be lethal.

God's holiness is his moral purity on steroids. We live in a fallen world. We are accustomed to sin and evil. But God is not. He hates sin. He is morally and spiritually allergic to it. I'm not talking about the big sins—adultery, murder, or drug addiction. I am talking about the respectable ones—lust, resentment, selfish ambition, unbelief, gossip, grumbling, self-centeredness, anger when life doesn't go my way, etc.

I was recently in Wenatchee, Washington. Their apple orchards make the state of Washington famous. Extending as far as I could see on either side of the highway were hundreds of orchards, thousands of trees, and hundreds of thousands of ripe apples. "I am going to stop and pick one," I told my wife.

"You can't do that," she said. "It's stealing."

"No one cares. There are millions of apples, and anyway, the orchards aren't fenced."

So, I pulled to the shoulder, picked an apple, and ate it shamelessly.

MARRIAGE IN PARADISE

This is what Adam and Eve did. They ate a piece of forbidden fruit. It wasn't murder. It wasn't adultery. It wasn't even drunkenness. They just ate fruit from a forbidden tree. Although we would consider this a minor infraction, God doesn't. Because he is holy, because he hates all shades of evil in a way that we cannot even imagine, his reaction was instantaneous and severe. He inflicted them with spiritual and physical death, banished them from his presence, drove them from the garden, and lest they thought he was joking or over-reacting, he placed an angel at the entrance with a flaming sword to strike down anyone trying to re-enter tainted with even the slightest sin. He afflicted Eve with pain in childbirth, and cursed the ground that he had commanded Adam to work. As we saw earlier, in Genesis 3:16 he also judged their relationship. Then he plunged the entire cosmos into death and decay, and if all of this was not enough, he judged Adam and Eve with original sin—an indwelling heart-pathology that expresses itself as pride and selfishness. We all inherit it at conception.

Obviously, sin does not bother us like it bothers God. We aren't holy. In fact, sin and evil—especially in ourselves—rarely offend us. So, we look at God's reaction and think, "unfair!" We assume that God grades on the curve, that those average or better get into heaven. But he doesn't. His standard is righteousness, i.e. moral perfection, and that is the one thing we universally lack.[1] Jesus summed up God's standard at the end of the Sermon on the Mount with this fearful verse, "You must be perfect as your heavenly father is perfect" (Matt. 5:48). Without this perfection, what Paul calls righteousness, we cannot enter heaven (get back into paradise).

God's reaction to evil didn't stop at Genesis 3. Genesis six introduced Noah's flood. Even the mothers and nursing babies died. In Genesis 19 fire and brimstone fell on Sodom and

The Gospel

Gomorrah. Again, women and infants were not excepted. We could go on and on.

Here is our universal problem. We are not holy. Therefore, it is very difficult for us to understand God. In addition, we lack righteousness. "None is righteous," Paul reminds us, "no, not one; no one understands, no one seeks God...no one does good, not even one" (Romans 3:10-12). Therefore, because God's standard is unattainable, and he is absolutely holy, he is at war with us. He is angry! "The wrath of God is being revealed from heaven against all the ungodliness and unrighteousness of men" (Romans 1:18).

But God is also love. That is why he doesn't want to be angry. It is also why he sent Jesus, his own Son, to save us from the "wrath to come" (1Thessalonians 1:10).

Although the bad news starts with God's holiness, it moves on to God's justice. His justice is holy. That means that, just as God hates evil in a way we can't understand, he is also infinitely and perfectly just in a way that we cannot imagine. Again, we are not like him. Once he has threatened a punishment, he can't just forgive and forget. To do so would be a compromise of his integrity. He would not be following through with his threats. For the Judge of the Universe, this would be sin, and God cannot sin nor even be tempted by sin. This means that God can only forgive after his justice has first been satisfied— after the transgressor has been punished. "We can only claim from him justice—and justice, for us, means certain condemnation," writes J. I. Packer. "God does not owe it to anyone to stop justice taking its course. He is not obliged to pity and pardon; if he does so it is an act done, as we say, 'of his own free will,' and nobody forces his hand. 'It does not depend on man's will or effort, but on God's mercy" (Rom 9:16 NEB).[2]

You have probably seen the statue of Lady Justice. Her form is engraved into the foot of the lamp posts before the U.S.

Supreme Court building. She wears a blindfold, (signifying impartial judging), rich or poor, celebrity or unknown—it doesn't matter. Her left hand holds a set of scales at eye level. The scales represent our deeds. The big question is this. What tips the scales, our virtues or vices? In her right hand is a sword, ready to punish everyone whose vices outweigh their virtues.

Lady Justice is not a perfect symbol of God for several reasons. God is not female. Also, God is so holy that only one small vice or sin is enough to completely tip the scales, outweighing any good we have done. In the words of R. C. Sproul—

> God is loving, but a major part of what He loves is His own perfect character, with a major aspect being the importance of maintaining justice and righteousness. Though God pardons sinners and makes great provision for expressing His mercy, *He will never negotiate His justice.* If we fail to understand that, the cross of Christ will be utterly meaningless to us.[3]

The repercussions of God's justice, coupled with his hatred of sin, are momentous. A day of final judgment is coming. On that day God will weigh us in his scales. For unbelievers, it will be a day of "wrath and fury" (Romans 2:8). The Bible describes us in our unconverted state as weak (Romans 5:6), ungodly (Romans 5:6), sinners (Romans 5:8), under God's wrath (Romans 5:9), and enemies (Romans 5:10), and, as we have already noted, impotent. Since none of us are righteous (perfect), and we need to be, we are in trouble. There is nothing human strength can do to save itself. "To be a Christian," notes Dave Harvey, "is to recognize that the only thing we have a perfect right to is the wrath of God—and that's not a right we want to insist on keeping."[4]

We have a problem. Since God's standard is perfection, no amount of trying harder will help. More sincerity won't help. More self-discipline is a waste of time. The solution to our problem lies outside of human effort. Should anyone be saved, God must do the saving!

THE GOOD NEWS

To anyone who really understands the bad news, the gospel is not just news. It is the best good news that anyone could possibly hear. When they hear it, like the homeless person under the bridge, they leap and shout for joy.

The good news begins with the truth that God is more than justice. He is also mercy and grace. He loves to forgive. But, humanly speaking, God has a problem: forgiveness and justice oppose each other, but God is both just and forgiving. So, how can he forgive at the expense of justice, i.e. without punishing the transgressor? To do so would compromise justice. How can he forgive us and punish us at the same time?

The answer to this problem is wonderful. "God so loved the world, that he gave his only Son, that whoever believes in him should not perish but have eternal life" (John 3:16). God looked down on humanity, his compassion and mercy were moved, his infinite wisdom designed a solution, and he acted. He sent his Son to die, not for friends, but enemies, to forgive the unforgivable so that he could reconcile us to himself, make us his friends, adopt us into his family, and simultaneously satisfy his justice. Here is how that happens.

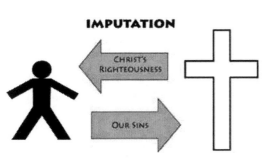

From Jesus-Is-Savior.com

Our faith in the gospel is like spiritual Velcro. It irrevocably unites us to Christ. That union causes two transactions to take place. First, our sins are transferred to Christ. Then, to satisfy God's justice, Jesus goes to the cross and receives the just punishment that you and I deserve. In our place, Jesus absorbs God's wrath. Adam and Eve deserved to be expelled from the Garden. In the same way, we deserve expulsion from God's presence. Therefore, to satisfy God's justice, and as our substitute, Jesus was forsaken. "My God, my God," he cried. "Why have you forsaken me?" All of this took place so that God could both forgive the unworthy and simultaneously satisfy the depths of his justice. Jesus experienced the torments that we deserve. Once God's justice was fully satisfied he was free to forgive. In the words of Romans 3:26, Jesus died so that God could be both "just and the justifier of the one who has faith in Jesus."

Our union with Christ produces a second transaction. It transfers Christ's righteousness to us. Remember, righteousness is the moral perfection that we need to enter heaven. "You must be perfect as your heavenly father is perfect" (Matt. 5:48). Jesus was the only righteous person, the only complete law-keeper, that has ever lived. He loved God with all his heart, all his soul, all his mind and all his strength. He also loved his neighbor as he wanted to be loved. He fulfilled God's law perfectly. Here is the wonderful truth. When we believe the gospel, God imputes Christ's law-keeping, to us. In other words, God "clothes" us with Christ's righteousness. Based on Christ's obedience, not our own, you and I become acceptable to God.

These two transactions were *infinitely* costly to God. It cost Christ the torments and sufferings that billions of sinners deserve. His pains are the measure of God's hatred of evil. But they are also the measure of the infinite depths of his incomprehensible love—love that Paul says, "*surpasses knowledge*" (Ephesians 3:19). With this in mind, the apostle John wrote these famous words, "God is love" (1 John 4:16).

The Gospel

Paul and John could make these extravagant statements about God's love for three reasons.

1st God's love is free. He does not owe it to anyone. He only owes us justice.

2nd God's love is for enemies.

3rd God has no need for the objects of his love.

The next chapter will explore these three propositions in depth and apply them to marriage.

Study Questions

- How would you explain the gospel to a non-Christian friend?
- In your own words, how would you sum up the bad news? Why is it necessary for a clear appreciation of the good news?
- In your own words, how would you sum up the good news?
- Based on this chapter, why do Christians sometimes use the term "double imputation" as a synonym for the gospel?
- How should a clear understanding of the gospel change how you relate to your spouse?
- After reading this chapter, what is God telling you to change?

SIX: Surpassing Knowledge

IN THE MODERN WORLD, love is a misunderstood concept. Since the sexual revolution of the sixties, it has become increasingly eroticized. For most people it means affection or an assertion of approval. "I love the way she talks to me." "I love the way he dresses and the way he exudes confidence." And, although God feels great affection, (and created eroticism), fundamentally love in the Bible is something much deeper, richer, and more powerful. When internalized, it transforms marriages.

As we noted at the end of the last chapter, in Ephesians 3:19 Paul says God's love "surpasses knowledge." It has three characteristics that make it so fantastic. We noted them at the close of chapter five.
- God's love is free
- God's love is for enemies
- God loves despite the complete lack of need for the beloved.

FREE LOVE

God's love is free! This means that God is free to give or not give it. Because no one is good enough to earn his love, God is not compelled to love. He owes love to no one. I remember the day I departed for my first year of college. "I love you," my mother said as she embraced me in a bear hug. "I am going to miss you." Tears flowed.

I felt her affection, and I was grateful. I hugged her back. "I love you, mom." But deep in my heart, I thought, *of course you love me I am your oldest son. You're my mom. Mom's love their kids. That's their job.*

Sometimes we mistakenly project this attitude onto God. When most of us read "God is love" (1Jn. 4:16), we think, *Of course. Isn't it God's job to be loving?* But, the Bible answers no!

God's first job is not to love but to be just. God does not owe us love, but he does owe us justice! If we were good enough to meet God's standards, then justice would obligate him to love or reward us. But Jesus is the only person that *merited* the Father's love. Therefore, he is the only person to whom God owes love. So, when God does love sinners, it is always free. It is never owed. God would be no less loving if he only gave us the justice we deserved.

But God *does* love us, and considering his freedom to not be loving, we should be astounded! Why? Because it would cost God *nothing* to be strictly just. But it was infinitely costly to love the undeserving.

Put yourself in God's place. Imagine that you had a servant who owed you for everything that he had and was, and yet rebelled against you, ignored you, despised you, and therefore only deserved your rejection and punishment. Then, realizing that it would be *infinitely* costly to love him, would you? Or would you just give him justice? If you are like me, probably justice. That is because we are not like God. Our love is not holy like God's. Human love is not the blazing, amazing, holy love revealed through the cross.

LOVE FOR ENEMIES

God's love surpasses knowledge for a second reason. It is love for enemies! We love those we like—those who love us back. Even members of the mafia show kindness to their friends. But God loves his *enemies*—those who don't love him back. Here is the astounding truth. God gives himself in extravagant love for those who have deeply offended him. He freely loves people he doesn't like.

Tim, one of the men in my church, spent five years in a California prison for armed robbery. While in prison he joined a Bible Study led by a man named Tex Watson. Tex was a member of the infamous Manson Family who savagely murdered the pregnant actress, Sharon Tate, and others in August of 1969. The next night they broke into the home of supermarket mogul, Leno La Bianca and his wife Rosemary. They heartlessly stabbed them multiple times watching them slowly bleed to death in great pain. Then with their blood, they wrote, "death to the pigs" and other obscene slogans on the walls.

Several years later, while serving a life sentence in prison, Watson was approached incognito by Susan LaBerge, Rosemary La Bianca's daughter. After she had built a relationship with him, she told Watson that she was LaBianca's daughter, that she was a Christian, and that she had come to forgive him for the cold-blooded murder of her mother and step-father. Susan's example eventually led to Watson's conversion. Watson shared his testimony with my friend, Tim, and it led to Tim's conversion as well. What motivated La Berge to extend such lavish forgiveness to the man who brutally murdered her family? God forgave her when she was his enemy, and that forgiveness motivated her to extend the same grace to her enemy, Tex Watson.

I was a Christian over fifteen years before I understood this. Like so many, I assumed that God sent his Son to die for me because he liked me. Therefore, I was only motivated to do the same—love and forgive those that I liked, not enemies. I assumed God's love in the same way that I assumed my mother's love. Therefore, I had little appreciation for it. But when I saw that God sent his Son to die for me when I was his reviled enemy everything changed.

What do we do with love like this? Not only is it uncommon, but it is also virtually nonexistent in our fallen world. Who do you know that would go to the cross for a friend, let alone an enemy? Love like this is only found, and that very imperfectly, amongst Christians like La Berge, who draw their spiritual nourishment from the rich compost of the gospel.

This is why Jesus instructed his disciples, "You have heard that it was said, 'You shall love your neighbor and hate your enemy.' But I say to you, *love your enemies* and pray for those who persecute you, so that you may be sons of your Father who is in heaven...You, therefore, must be perfect as your heavenly Father is perfect" (Matthew 5:43-44, 48).

As we have already noted, even unbelievers love their friends. If all we do is love those whom we like how are we different from the world? The acid test of true Christianity, what points to new birth, is *the willingness to forgive and love enemies.*

This willingness to love an enemy is vital to marriage. Are you willing to forgive your spouse? Are you willing to go out to your spouse in love despite his or her imperfections, despite the numerous ways he or she has hurt you? Only Christians impacted by gospel-love will try to do this. Our love is always a response to God's love. Orthodoxy—right belief—always precedes orthopraxy—right behavior. "We love because he first loved us" (1 Jn. 4:19).

LOVE WITHOUT NEED

God's love surpasses knowledge for a third and final reason. He doesn't need our love. When Moses encountered God for the first time in the burning bush he looked "and behold, the bush was burning, yet *it was not consumed*" (Exodus 3:2). In this passage God is represented by a fire that needs no fuel. What energized the flame was something internal to the flame itself. It was a flame burning on itself. It was a flame without need.

When Moses asked the being represented by the flame for his name, God responded, "I AM WHO I AM...Say this to the people of Israel: I AM has sent me to you" (Exodus 3:14). God was communicating one powerful message. I just AM. I always have been and always will be. I need nothing outside of myself. I am completely self-satisfied and self-sufficient.

This points to one simple truth: God has no needs! He doesn't even need to exercise love. In fact, we have nothing that God needs. The big word for this is God's aseity. Aseity just means "self-existent," or existing "without need." A being with aseity is complete in himself. He lacks nothing. He lacks no happiness. He lacks no fellowship. He is never lonely because he is, and always has been, in constant communion with the other members of the Trinity. In fact, God possesses infinite eternal happiness within himself. "Infinite" means that it would be impossible for him to be happier. "Infinite" also means nothing can disturb his happiness. "God is self-sustaining," observes Norman Geisler, "and does not need anything, but everything needs him."[1] In the words of Paul, "Who has given a gift to God that he might be repaid?" (Romans 11:35).

MARRIAGE IN PARADISE

My parents sent me to a Roman Catholic grade school. One day one of the students raised the question of ultimate purpose, "Why did God create people?" The sincere nun responded, "God created you because he was lonely. He needed friendship."

This was how I saw it until my mid-thirties. As I began to understand the God of the Bible I realized that nothing could be further from the truth. God is "not served by human hands as though *he needed anything*" (Acts 17:25).

"God is supremely independent of the world," notes theologian, Bruce Ware, "and hence he *simply does not need the world he has made*. His transcendence is revealed most clearly by his independent and infinite self-sufficiency."[2]

So, if we are God's enemies, and he does not owe us love, but only justice, and he has absolutely no need for us, what rational motive can we possibly ascribe to God for the gospel? Remember, our salvation was *infinitely* costly. Why was God's Son willing to descend to earth and suffer the horrors of the judgment we deserve on the cross for creatures who could do nothing to advance his happiness? We have no rational answer except the simple biblical proposition.

"God is love" (1 Jn. 4:16).

Can you now understand why Paul wrote that God's love surpasses knowledge (Ephesians 3:19)? Compared to human love, God's love is unique and superlative in its "breadth and length and height and depth" (Ephesians 3:18). Human love does not love enemies to whom it only owes justice. Human love doesn't make extravagant sacrifices for those who return its love with hate (John 15:18, 25). Human love does not love despite the complete absence of need. Need is foundational to everything we do. In fact, we are so needy that we can't even imagine acting without need (Try it and see if you don't agree). We love God because we need him. We need his help. We need his approval. We need salvation. We need happiness, and he is the source. We love people because we need them, or at least we need God's approval for loving them. Our love is never disinterested.

I recently heard the true story about a Christian couple that had been married ten years. One day the husband confessed that he was having an affair. To save face with their friends, he asked his wife to go along with him. He begged her to continue acting as though they were happily married even though he was spending his weekends with his new mistress. He was living a lie, and he wanted her to help him cover it up.

To her credit, she said "no" and moved out. Naturally, she was filled with bitterness. She resented her husband, and none of us would blame her. First, he callously betrayed her, then he tried to selfishly use her. He was utterly indifferent to her happiness or welfare. When my friend told me that she detested him I sympathized.

Now imagine that your spouse has done something similar. Then imagine yourself so happy that it would be impossible for reconciliation to make you happier. Imagine that you had no obligation to do anything but exact justice. Then imagine feeling such a passion for his or her happiness that you were willing to take the justice that he or she deserved (crucifixion) for the way they treated you, in order to get reconciled—and all of this while lacking any need for them? It was all for their happiness, not yours. This is just a glimpse of how holy, uncommon, and astoundingly wonderful God's love is. It is utterly unselfish. There is no "me" in it. In our fallen world, this kind of love only exists where the gospel has gone deep, and even then, it is mixed with base motives.

SO WHAT?

What does this have to do with marriage? Everything!

First, when husbands and wives understand the bad news and the good news, they give up on earning God's love or acceptance by how they relate to each other. They rejoice in

MARRIAGE IN PARADISE

God's commands, and they try to walk them out, but when they fail they rest secure in his mercy, grace, and love. Their failure to love, support, submit to, or respect their spouse does not change their standing with God. They are justified by faith alone. They do everything possible to live a life pleasing to God, but they completely reject PBA (performance-based acceptance). Instead, they live in the glorious freedom provided by the gospel.

Second, the reality of the gospel means that couples no longer define love by their *feelings*. One of the most common grounds for divorce is "I just don't love him/her anymore." But this assumes that love is a feeling. Feelings of affection are a fruit of love, but they are not at the heart of divine love. God's love is something much deeper.

If God's love was primarily a feeling, we would all be damned forever. But just the opposite is true. God loved us with action when he didn't even like us. *He died for his enemies.* The gospel reminds us that true love greatly transcends feelings. The gospel says: love is a verb! It's alright to dislike your spouse. We all feel that way at times. In fact, we are most like God when we go out in love to a spouse that we don't like. For Christians, it is never OK to refuse to love a spouse because we don't like them.

We often hear statements like, "My spouse has disappointed me. If I knew they were going to be like this I would have never married him or her." Maybe she gained weight, or he is not the provider you expected? Maybe you or your spouse are going through a time of deep depression. The gospel says, "How you feel about your spouse is irrelevant." Why? Again, when you were most unlovable, when God's wrath rested upon you, when you had deeply disappointed him, Jesus paid an *infinite price* for you. If that is true, then we are duty bound to love the person closest to us the same way.

Third, these gospel truths mean we don't approach our marital commitments with self at the center. One of the most common reasons for divorce goes like this. "I owe it to myself to be happy! I know God wants me to be happy. This marriage is not making me happy, so I am going to move on. I'm going to find someone that will make me happy." This is a worldview with self at the center. But the gospel is all about *death to self*. It is about serving. It is about "swearing to our own hurt, and not changing" (Ps. 15:4). If Jesus thought this way, we would all perish. But, he did just the opposite. He aggressively put the me-centered life to death. We must do the same.

Fourth, as we saw in the last chapter, the gospel bumps the husband's love to a transcendent level. "Husbands love your wives as *Christ loved his church* and *gave himself up for her*" (Ephesians 5:25). A rational husband, who really understands the gospel, will be thinking, "Lord, this is impossible. I can't do this." If you aren't thinking this way it proves that you are either incredibly arrogant, or you don't get the gospel yet.

But, although he knows it is impossible, he also knows that he is indwelt by God's Spirit, and that this same Spirit is the one who communicates God's love to him. He knows that in this life he will never perfect God's love. That awaits eternity. But he also knows that he can grow in his capacity to love like Christ.

Not only does the gospel demonstrate what God's love looks like, it also motivates husbands to apply it. For the first fifteen years of my marriage, I assumed that God loved me because I was so sincere, because I tried so hard. I knew I was a sinner. I believed in justification by faith alone, but I didn't see God's holiness or the depth of my sinfulness. The result was predictable. Since I assumed that God loved me because I performed, I loved Judy to the degree that she performed.

However, as I began to go deeper with the gospel, I began to grapple with my sinfulness, God's holiness, his justice, and what I deserved. The more I did, the more my love changed. I saw that God didn't love me because I performed. Just the opposite. He loved me despite the complete absence of saving performance. When his only obligation to me was justice, he sent his Son to take the punishment that I deserved.

That changed everything. How can I, who am so unworthy, receive this kind of love from God and not try to give it to the person living closest to me? When a husband is not attempting to love his spouse this way it points to one thing—he doesn't really get the gospel—or worse, he doesn't care. In either case, it points to a profound form of spiritual dementia. It might even mean a failure to launch—the absence of new birth.

Fifth, the gospel models what submission looks like for wives. "Wives, submit to your husbands as to the Lord...in everything" (Ephesians 5:22,24). Paul can command this because, as we have seen, in the gospel Jesus submitted to his Father (and human authorities) perfectly. "My food is to do the will of him who sent me" (John 4:34). "My Father is working until now, and I am working too" (John 5:17). "I always do what pleases Him" (John 8:29). This doesn't mean that Jesus didn't have his own will. Remember, in the Garden of Gethsemane he pleaded with the Father to bypass the cross. But when the Father said, "No," he submitted joyfully.

In the same way, no woman really knows if she has a Christlike submissive attitude until she is willing to have a submissive attitude toward an imperfect husband, one who sometimes leads selfishly. Remember, Jesus submitted to selfish leadership. He submitted to Pilate, a brutal, self-centered, cruel dictator. This never means submitting to physical or verbal abuse, but it does mean a submissive *attitude* toward your husband's office, even though sometimes exercised unjustly (1 Peter 2:18-23).

CONCLUSION

Summing up the husband and wife's roles: every husband who really sees Jesus absorbing God's wrath in his place, even though he only deserves God's righteous anger, and despite the fact that God had absolutely no need for him, will be forever motivated to love his wife the same way.

Any wife who sees the depths of Christ's submission to all authority, in order to save her, will desire to submit herself to her husband's imperfect authority.

Stephen Charnock (1628-80) taught theology at Oxford during the Puritan era. He is one of history's great Christian thinkers. Here is how he framed his understanding of the cross.

> We cannot look upon Christ crucified for us, for our guilt, and consider that we had deserved all that he suffered, and that he suffered not by our entreaty, nor by any obligation from us, but merely from his own love, but the meditation of this must... *melt us into sorrow.*[3]

In the next chapters we will examine what it looks like in a routine marriage to have the gospel "melt us into sorrow," and we will watch as God transforms our marriages, taking them closer and closer back to his Genesis 2 paradise.

STUDY QUESTIONS

- Paul wrote that God's love "surpasses knowledge" (Ephesians 3:17). What did you learn from this chapter that would cause you to agree?
- When Christians say that God's love is "free" what do they mean?
- John 3:16 reads "God so loved the world that he gave his only begotten Son," but (1 Thessalonians. 1:10) says "Jesus who delivers us from the wrath to come." What is it, love or wrath? And how does my answer impact my marriage?
- God loves without having any need. Can you think of a time when you have done something without some need motivating it?
- As you think about God's love for yourself, what do you need to change to begin loving your spouse this way?

SEVEN: The School of Christ

ON OCTOBER 31, 1517 Martin Luther trustingly nailed ninety-five theses to the door of a church in Wittenberg, Germany. In the spiritual world, behind the scenes, momentous changes occurred. The Western world has never been the same.

Another important, but less celebrated event, took place almost eight years later. On June 27, 1525 Martin married Katherine von Bora. The groom was 41 and the bride 26. Martin admitted that he wasn't infatuated with Katie, or she with him. They barely knew each other. Yet, their marriage was such a success that, in the words of Luther's biographer, Roland Bainton, it did more than any other marriage "to determine the tone of German domestic relations for the next four centuries."[1]

MARRIAGE IN PARADISE

Their marriage began unconventionally. In 1523 twelve nuns at a local convent took up the cause of the Reformation. They wanted to escape, move to Wittenberg, and join Luther and company. But in the 16th century, escape from a convent was a capital offense. Luther persuaded a local merchant, who regularly delivered barrels of herring to the convent, to put the twelve in empty barrels and smuggle them out. They arrived at Wittenberg in the middle of the night. Luther now had the onerous job of finding them husbands, which he did for all but one.

The last remaining unmarried nun was Katherine von Bora. Twice Luther had arranged a marriage for her, and twice the negotiations had fallen apart. In frustration, Katie said that she would take Luther himself. It was a joke because she, and everyone else, knew that Luther was completely beyond her reach. Luther passed the joke on to his father, but Martin's father took it seriously. He reminded his now famous son of two things. First, he wanted grandchildren, and second, for that to happen his son needed a wife.

A few weeks later Martin and Katie were engaged. Inviting his friend, Spalatin, to the wedding, Luther wrote, "You must come to my wedding. I have made the angels laugh and the devils weep."[2] On their wedding day neither Martin nor Katie suspected that theirs was a match made in heaven.

Marriage to Katie turned Luther's life upside down. She gave birth to six children, one every two years for twelve years. (Two died in infancy). In addition, after the death of close relatives, Martin and Katie adopted their four children. Last, because the Elector Frederick gave them the Augustinian cloister as a wedding present, and they had many vacant rooms, students began arriving to board with them and sit under Martin's teaching.

Katie was the industrious, frugal, business minded Proverbs thirty-one woman. She brought Martin "good and not harm all the days of his life" (Proverbs 31:12). In the 16th century, a household of this size, often twenty-five or more, required many servants. All of this Katie oversaw and managed with great skill, leaving Martin free to pursue his theological studies and voluminous writing. In addition, she brewed the family beer, managed a pond from which she netted trout, carp, pike, and perch, maintained their orchard, took care of their livestock, (slaughtering them herself), and homeschooled their children. One biographer wrote, "Kate became gardener, fisher, brewer, fruit grower, cattle and horse breeder, cook, bee-keeper, provisioner, nurse, and vintner. In 1542, for example, the Luther's had five cows, nine calves, one goat, two kids, eight pigs, two sows, and three piglets."[3]

Martin's favorite book of the Bible was Galatians. So deep did his love for Katie grow that he nicknamed it his Katherine von Bora. He depended upon her. They were a team. There is an old saying: behind every successful man is a capable and supportive wife. That was Katie. Martin's literary output during this time was herculean. Little of it would have occurred without Katie von Bora.

Like most successful marriages, there were stresses and strains. For both Katie and Martin marriage was the school of Christ. One stress was money. Martin had been a Roman Catholic monk for twenty years. As a single man he owned nothing but his books and the clothes on his back. Because he saw poverty as a virtue, he was in the habit of giving his money away. In fact, his giving was so extravagant, and well-known, that the local banker and artist, Cranach, refused his drafts. Now that he had a wife and family, this attitude was a problem.

Katie was Luther's opposite. She was frugal. She was shrewd in the stewardship of money, and she was down to earth. Martin was the most popular author in Europe. Anything he wrote sold thousands of copies. Yet, Martin

MARRIAGE IN PARADISE

refused to take royalties. Because of this the printers made a fortune from his writing. Rightfully, this upset Katie. They had a large household to feed, and they never had enough money. "Martin, please charge royalties. We are in desperate need of cash," she must have pleaded. There were fireworks. Luther had to change, and the changes came slowly and painfully.

Communication was another tension. At the end of a long day of study, teaching up to four classes, meeting with dignitaries, and counseling the wayward Martin was exhausted. The last thing he wanted to do was talk to Katie. But Katie would have none of it.

Sometimes Martin was impatient with Katie. He would be hard at work in his study, concentrating intensely, and Katie would enter asking about some trivial piece of information. "Is the King of Prussia related to the Grand Duke?" Luther was often tempted to explode, especially when there were several interruptions like this in a row.

Martin's lack of cleanliness also aggravated Katie. On their wedding night she discovered that the straw in Luther's bed had not been changed in over a year. It was rotting in his sweat.

Then there were all the normal irritations experienced by every married couple. Once at the dinner table when Luther was in the middle of answering a student's question, "Katie broke in, 'Doctor, why don't you stop talking and eat?'

"'I wish,' snapped Luther, 'that women would repeat the Lord's Prayer before opening their mouths.' The students tried to get him back on track again," notes Luther's biographer, "but he was derailed for [the rest of] that meal."[4] Because Katie was strong-willed, submission to her husband was not always easy. There were fireworks. Nevertheless, she grew in her ability to be submissive in attitude.

THE SCHOOL OF CHRIST

For Martin and Katie, marriage was the school of Christ. Prior to the Reformation, the marital state was considered inferior to celibacy. The celibate life was ultimate. Pre-reformation Christians saw the monastery or convent, not marriage, as the school of Christ. Because salvation was earned, those who really wanted to grow in godliness became a monk or nun.

But justification by faith alone changed all of that. If salvation could not be earned, if it was a free gift of grace, the rigors of the monastic life were no longer a spiritual advantage. Several years into marriage God opened Martin's eyes: marriage to Katie was the *real* "school of Christ."

Why did Martin call marriage the school of Christ? Katie was the person he loved and needed most, but she was also the person that aggravated him most. These circumstances, and others, forced Martin and Katie to face their indwelling sin. As they tried to live out Ephesians five they quickly learned that they couldn't do it without supernatural aid. They saw their utter bankruptcy.

This is the point of Gary Thomas' book *Sacred Marriage*. The subtitle reads, W*hat If God Designed Marriage To Make Us Holy More Than To Make Us Happy?* The subtitle is a bit of an oxymoron. I am sure Thomas would agree. You can't separate holiness from happiness. Holy people are increasingly happy people. However, the initial shock of self-denial, self-criticism, and sense of moral failure which accompanies growth in holiness, often hinders short-term happiness. The pain causes couples to ask. "What is wrong?" Thomas answers, "Nothing!" God is after your holiness. Hang on. It will get better.

He relates the advice Francis De Sales gave a young lady, deeply in love, who felt guilty because she was getting married. Was it the easy way out? Shouldn't she care for her ailing father, and after his death, devote herself to the celibate life?

Marriage seemed utopian—a selfish choice. DeSales, a Catholic, gave her an unexpected answer. "The state of marriage is one that requires more virtue and constancy than any other. It is a perpetual exercise of *mortification*. From this Thyme plant, despite the bitter nature of its juice, you may be able to draw and make the honey of a holy life."[5]

Marriage is not the easy way. Far from it! Marriage is a perpetual spiritual workout. It is as deeply rewarding as it is at times stressful and difficult. Thomas compares marriage to a spiritual gym "in which our capacity to experience and express God's love is strengthened and further developed" as we push our spiritual muscles to the breaking point.[6]

TRANSITION TO THE PERSONAL

This chapter begins the second section of *Marriage In Paradise.* The first part discussed the ultimate purpose of marriage. We looked at it through the lens of creation, fall, and redemption. We discussed the ways married couples relate differently from other people. Married couples relate to each other structurally, and God wants us to love each other in that context. The husband is the head. His duty is sacrificial love. God charges his wife to submit to, encourage, and respect his headship. In this way, their love is unique.

But couples also love each other personally. God commands us to love our spouse just as we would any other relative, friend, or church member. That requires humility, unselfishness, loyalty, the rejection of idolatry, godly speech, etc. It means shouldering responsibilities and renouncing rights. These will be the subjects of the remaining chapters.

The last chapter will discuss sex. It is a third way couples love each other, and it is the second way they love uniquely. I have put it in its own chapter at the end. The ability to love unselfishly makes for great sex. (That is why the above-mentioned chapters come first). Great sex doesn't produce unselfishness. Unselfishness produces great sex. Good sex does not make the marriage. Good sex is the fruit of a good marriage.

As always, understanding and applying the gospel is the key. As we look at specific sins that obstruct our ability to love unselfishly, we will gain an understanding of how the gospel helps us overcome them. If we can serve our spouse unselfishly, we can serve just about anyone.

THE GOAL?

The goal of the school of Christ is spiritual maturity. A couple of years after my conversion, in my early twenties, my brother and I went to a men's Bible study. The leader, Sam, was a missionary home from the Far East. Because he was in his mid-forties, he seemed old and mature. As we walked away, I remember my brother turning and saying something like this—"Can you imagine what we are going to be like in twenty years—in our mid-forties—so empowered by the Holy Spirit that most of our sins and weaknesses will have disappeared?" At the time I agreed with my brother, but we were both wrong. Years have passed, and I now know that this is not how sanctification works.

The experience of spiritual maturity is not a feeling of increasing conquest, competence, or ability. It is downward. Growing humility is the first sign of spiritual maturity. The fruits are an increasing sense of my utter sinfulness, complete bankruptcy, inability to love anyone without God's help, failure to merit God's love in any sense, and a desperate need for the grace that comes through the gospel. Spiritual maturity is growth in dependence. In other words, spiritual growth means feeling more sinful, more dependent, and more thankful for God's awesome, unearnable redeeming love. And, the more unworthy we feel, the sweeter God's love becomes.

MARRIAGE IN PARADISE

Jonathan Edwards stated it more powerfully. He suggested that *everything* (not some things, but everything) the Holy Spirit does is to enhance that sense of need, dependence, and humility.

> [Humility] is a great and most essential thing in true religion. The *whole* frame of the gospel, and *everything* appertaining to the new covenant, and *all* God's dispensations towards fallen man, are calculated to bring to pass this effect in the hearts of men. They that are destitute of [humility], have no true religion, whatever profession they may make, and how high so ever their religious affections may be.[7]

This was the apostle Paul's experience. In 1 Corinthians 15:9 he said, "I am the *least of the apostles*." About five years later, he wrote to the church at Ephesus, "I am the l*east of all the saints*" (Ephesians 3:8). At the end of his life he wrote Timothy that he was *"the foremost of sinners"* (1 Timothy 1:15). Paul was not exaggerating. That was how he really felt. In his own eyes, he had descended from the least of the apostles, to the least of all the saints, to the foremost of sinners. For Paul, spiritual maturity meant feeling less confident, less adequate, and less capable while simultaneously feeling more loved by God.

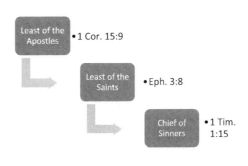

Attempting to live a biblical marriage is a key to discovering this for yourself. It won't happen until you submit to the Lordship of Christ and *really decide* to obey God. Submitting to Christ's lordship means a resolve to love God with all your heart, soul, mind, and strength, and your neighbor as yourself. And who is your closest neighbor? Your spouse! And who is often the hardest person to love? Your spouse.

For married couples, obedience means a single-minded decision to walk out Ephesians five, verse 22 to 33. All who have really tried have learned that they can't, at least not consistently. Marriage humbles us, and that is God's intention. Above all other truths, the school of Christ teaches us our moral and spiritual bankruptcy.

When a woman makes up her mind to submit to her husband "as unto Christ," what happens? She discovers the depths of her unbelief, her desire to control, and her selfishness. Maddie is a good example. She homeschooled her three children for seven years, but Jacob, the oldest, was now fourteen and becoming increasingly difficult. She could no longer handle him. Her husband, Ken, tried to intervene, but nothing worked. For three months Maddie and Ken discussed all the alternatives. Private school was out. They couldn't afford it. It was now August, and a decision had to be made. "We've tried everything," Ken said. "I believe God wants us to send Jacob to public school. Let's try it for six months and watch him carefully. If things get worse, we'll reconsider."

Maddie wanted to submit to Ken as unto Christ and trust God to work through him. But she took counsel with her fears. What if Jacob falls in with the wrong crowd? What about pot? What if a hot girl comes on to him? Worse, what if she starts sexting him?[8] She argued with Ken. She withdrew. She became depressed. She knew she was supposed to trust God, but she couldn't. She wanted the steering wheel, she wanted control. She was discovering the depth of her sin.

In the same way, Ken wanted to love Maddie "as Christ loved the church." He wanted to be the servant leader described in Ephesians 5:25. It all sounded so noble, so altruistic. But, it wasn't that easy. The more he tried to love

MARRIAGE IN PARADISE

Maddie, the harder it got. She became bitter. She withdrew. He was hurt. Jesus died for his enemies. Why couldn't he? He wanted to serve her despite his feelings, but it just wasn't in him. Instead of going out to her in love, he found himself also withdrawing. He wanted to forgive, but it was coming slowly if at all.

But behind the scenes God was at work using their failings for their good. God knew Ken and Maddie's limitations. He knew full well what they could and couldn't do, and in mercy he was using their marriage to introduce them to themselves, to draw them into a place of humility, dependence, and need—a place of real maturity. They didn't know it, but they were in the school of Christ.

Mature Christians are those who have experienced their personal bankruptcy, and their marriage is one of the tools that God used to help them experience it. They now cling to Christ in a new way. They know what they deserve, and they live by faith in the amazing grace provided by the gospel. The new knowledge of their personal bankruptcy also makes them appreciate God's mercy, grace, and love in a new way.

In closing, Luther was right. Marriage is the school of Christ. It rubs our spiritual noses in our selfishness. It teaches us perseverance. It forces us to make someone else's priorities more important than our own. As that happens, as we discover how weak we really are, the glory of Christ gets brighter and brighter. We love him more. We need him more. Our compassion for the failings of others grows. And that is what moving into maturity looks and feels like.

For these reasons, and others, it is crucial that we give ourselves to obeying Paul's clear instructions in Ephesians 5. Then we need to walk in thankfulness for our mate, our marriage, and God's kindness as our weakness exposes our moral and spiritual bankruptcy.

STUDY QUESTIONS
- Is the idea of Christian maturity, as described in this chapter, new to you? If so, how did this chapter change your understanding of it?
- Have you ever really committed to single-mindedly living out Ephesians 5:22-33? Why or why not?
- Has your marriage already exposed some of your sins and failings? If so, how have you responded? How should you respond?
- What has your relationship with your spouse taught you about your virtues? Your sins and weaknesses?

EIGHT: Gospel Humility

ADAM'S SIN DRASTICALLY affected himself, Eve, and their descendants. Theologians call that affect Original Sin—a corruption of human nature, causing it to turn away from God and in upon self. It is a form of self-worship. One key way that Original Sin affects our relationship with other people is pride or hubris. In the words of Augustine, "The soul abandons Him to whom it ought to cleave as its end and becomes a kind of end to itself."[1] Theologian Anthony Hoekema sums it up succinctly. "Sin is at root a form of pride."[2]

The conflict between Adam and Eve described in Genesis 3:16—a symptom of this moral and spiritual corruption—was an ongoing struggle for control. "To the woman he said… 'Your desire shall be contrary to your husband, but he shall rule over you'" (Genesis 3:16). In chapter four we learned that Paul wrote Ephesians 5:22-33 to help couples overcome this judgment as they begin began the road back to God's marital paradise.

The subject of Chapters 8, 9, and 10 is pride, how it affects couples, and how to overcome it.

ORIGINAL SIN

Pride is the idolatry of self. Instead of a child, spouse, or money, I worship me. It is the religion of "me-ism." A friend summed it up with this transparent confession, "My whole life has been a search for a pedestal on which to place a statue of myself." In a similar moment of transparency, another added, "My sin is simple: I just want everyone to worship me." These people confessed what few of us have the courage to admit. It sounds so perverse, but when we are honest, we will admit that, deep down inside, this is how most of us feel most of the time.

Pride is the heart deception that I am god, or at least should be. I am the center of my own personal universe. It is all about me. Everything should revolve around me. I am the most important person in the room. I make up my own rules. Pride drives fallen human nature. And although it is generally hidden from us, it is the assassin of marital happiness.

In my book, *Gospel Powered Humility* (P&R 2011) I argue that every vice flows from the fountain of pride, just as every virtue flows from humility. Because humility considers others more important than itself, humility is foundational to love. Jesus was humble: he made us more important than himself, and Philippians exhorts us to imitate him. "In humility count others more significant [more important] than yourselves" (Philippians 2:3b). The most important "other" to elevate this way is the spouse with whom you sleep and live.

Remember, 1 Corinthians 13, the famous love chapter? It reminds us that love is the test of spiritual authenticity. It is the crucial measure of our spiritual progress, and my willingness to humble myself and derive my happiness from the happiness of my spouse is the measure of my love. In other words, my love is most like God's when I make the needs, desires, and wants of my spouse more important than my own—especially when my spouse is not at his or her best or is disagreeable.

Notice, humility is not just thinking bad thoughts about myself. It is thinking more highly about my mate. In fact, Tim Keller reminds us that really humble people rarely think about self at all.[3] But when they do it is realistic. They know that they are more deeply flawed than they ever imagined, but they also know that the opposite is true: they are more deeply loved than they ever imagined.

Therefore, humble people are content, thankful, and at rest. By contrast, proud people think they deserve better, and they are convinced they are not getting it. It makes them grumpy, discontent, and ungrateful. But humble people think they are always getting better than they deserve. For these reasons, and more, humble people are happy people, even as their proud friends are increasingly miserable.

Our love will be according to our humility. In fact, the growing sense of bankruptcy and sinfulness, discussed in the last chapter, dilutes the poison of sin's pride, freeing us to love with increasing vitality. Those returning to God's paradise "hitch" a ride on humility's wagon. Here are some examples of what humility looks like.

Your spouse likes Italian, but you like seafood. Humility elevates the spouse and their desires, and love finds an Italian restaurant. But pride clings to its rights: it demands seafood.

Your spouse likes to vacation at the shore, but you prefer the mountains. Humility makes the spouse's desires more important, and then love reserves a place at the seashore. Pride insists on the mountains.

Your spouse is more cautious, and it irritates you. Humility makes your spouse more important, and love acts cautiously for the sake of the spouse. The examples are endless.

The point of this chapter is that, besides the order that God so richly values (Chapters I-IV), nothing is more crucial to your long-term happiness than the pursuit of humility, and the love that follows, and *we get our humility at the foot of the cross.*

In chapter five we learned that the gospel strips us of our delusions of self-importance. It reminds us that we deserve nothing from God but judgment. It makes grumblers thankful. It softens hard hearts. It turns users into servants. It renders critics compassionate. It reduces people that demand their rights into yielding servants. The gospel transforms selfish ambition into ambition for the success of my spouse. It changes bitter people into forgivers, and condescenders into admires.

The pursuit of humility effectively kicks eighty percent of our marital problems to the curb, and again, looking hard at Christ's humility, demonstrated by the gospel, is where we acquire this virtue.

DEFINITIONS

We need to pause for definitions. By pride I mean the inability to see myself for who I really am, and the parallel inability to see God for who he really is. Its symptom is self-flattery, the assumption, seldom admitted, that the problem is external to me, that I am a really good person, more virtuous and more sincere than most. This is what David had in mind when he wrote, "For in his own eyes he [the fool] flatters himself too much to detect or hate his sin" (Ps. 36:2 NIV).

That is why pride is spiritual blindness. The greater my pride the more unaware of it I will be. A proud person considers her virtue great, and her sin small. This inflated opinion blinds her to pride's presence. Pride is a patch on the eye of the heart, making accurate self-appraisal impossible. The proud person cannot see their vices, and the vice to which they are most blind is their pride.

This means irony: the proud person thinks they are humble, but the humble person thinks they are proud. So, if you are thinking *I don't need humility*, if you are thinking, *I wish I could get my spouse to read this,* be warned. It is a sure symptom that you have the eye patch on.

A few years after my conversion I read C. S. Lewis' *Mere Christianity.* I remember coming to chapter eight, "The Great Sin." It was about pride. Several times in the chapter Lewis indicated that the evidence of pride is that a proud person thinks they are humble. Then he ends the chapter, "If you think you are not conceited, it means you are very conceited indeed."[4] I remember thinking, *Well, I don't think I am conceited. I actually think I am pretty humble, certainly more than average.* However, deep down inside I knew his words had the ring of authenticity. I sensed he was right even though I didn't see it, so I prayed, "God help me see the truth of Lewis' words." That was forty years ago, and God has been faithful to answer that prayer. Maybe that is you. Maybe you are reading this chapter and responding like I did. Go to God in prayer. It is one he loves to answer.

Here is how Jonathan Edwards, considered by many to be America's greatest theologian, described the humble saint.

> [A humble] saint is not apt to think himself eminent in anything; all his graces and experiences are ready to appear to him to be comparatively small; but especially his humility. There is nothing that appertains to Christian experience, and true piety, that is so much out of his sight as his humility. He is a thousand times more quick-sighted to discern his pride than his humility: that he easily discerns, and is apt to take much notice of, but hardly discerns his humility. On the contrary, the deluded hypocrite,

that is under the power of spiritual pride, is so blind to nothing as his pride; and so quick-sighted to nothing, as the shows of humility that are in him.[5]

Pride is systemic to the human condition. It is what we are by nature. No one is completely free from it. Every time a sperm and egg unite, a proud creature comes into eternal existence. Only the gospel is strong enough to humble it.

Humility is the opposite. It begins as we see self in God's light—-"wretched, pitiable, poor, blind, and naked" (Revelation 3:17). The gospel, centered on the cross, convinces me that I am much more sinful then I ever thought, even as it also convinces me that I am much more loved and valued than I could have ever thought.

Heaven will be toxic to pride. Why? We will see God as he is, and in his light we will see ourselves as we really are. "Now I know in part, then I shall know fully, even as I have been fully known" (1 Corinthians 13:12b). What will I "know?" I will know myself as God knows me with all my warts and blemishes. I will see how utterly unlovable I was, and I will spend eternity overwhelmed by the grace and goodness of the God who went to the cross and suffered infinite pains to save me anyway.

Humility is liberating. It makes couples happy and content. Humble marriages are happy marriages. Humility is a spiritual teeter-totter. As I go down my spouse can't help but go up. Humble people think about their spouse more and about self less. The more they see their spouse's virtues, and their personal vices, the more they think their virtues small and their spouse's great.

The manifestations of pride are many. They include, but are not limited to, looking down on your mate, impatience with his or her weaknesses, irritability, inability to hear criticism (self-justification), demanding your rights, selfish ambition,

Gospel Humility

inability to forgive, condescending speech, and a lack of gratitude.

Your ability to sustain a deep and abiding personal affection for your spouse, romance if you will, will be according to your pursuit of humility.

HUMILITY AND SANCTIFICATION

If all of this is true, then it follows that God sanctifies us by leading us into deeper levels of humility. We saw how Jonathan Edwards believed that the level of our humility is the measure of our godliness.

Here is a test to help us discern our progress. What would your spouse say about your humility? You can hide your arrogance from your Sunday congregation. You can hide it from coworkers. You can hide it from your extended family, but you can't hide it from the one person who lives and sleeps with you 24x7. Daily he or she tastes the fruit of your growing humility or its absence. In their excellent book, *The Prideful Soul's Guide to Humility,* the authors observe—

> Because my pride is generally the quiet kind, some people are fooled. My wife is not; she knows me. If I am going to deal with pride in my life, I have to keep dealing with it at home, for *the way we are at home is the way we really are.*[6]

Here is a powerful truth. It is one to linger on. "The way we are at home" when the door is closed to the outside world, and no one is there to watch, "is the way we really are." So, what would your spouse say? The remainder of this chapter, and the next two, will ask eight questions to help you evaluate the level of your humility.

Examine yourself. Read these with your spouse and, if courageous enough, ask for his or her critique. Don't react defensively. Every person reading this chapter, including this author, is a proud sinner that needs to grow in humility. That is the only kind of person Christ saves. If Edwards is right, that everything God does with us is to humble us, then your spouse's critique is a wonderful opportunity to enter more deeply into the life of Christ.

QUESTION 1—WHOSE SIN ARE YOU FOCUSED ON?

There is an old saying. You can't change other people. This is especially true of your spouse. Only God can do that. *The only person you can change is yourself.* Despite this, in marriage counselling, most spouses come with 20/20 clarity about their spouse's failings, but only 20/500 about their own. Most people come to marriage counseling to fix their spouse.

Janice and John had been married twenty-five years, but their marriage was unravelling. When I asked Janice to describe the problem, she launched into a ten-minute critique of John. He didn't listen. He wasn't attentive. He was too interested in sex. He often didn't make it home for dinner. Had he committed adultery? No! Had he beaten her? No! Was he failing to provide for their large family? No! Was he withholding sex? No! Nevertheless, all she could see were her husband's failings.

Did he need to change? Yes. Were many of her complaints valid? Yes. But that was not the issue. When I asked where she had failed, she gave me a blank look as if to say, *Have you lost your mind? What kind of questions is that? Can't you see, It's all John's fault.* But it was obvious after five minutes of listening, that Janice also had "issues," that they were a major contribution to their marital problems, and that to them she was completely blind. All she could see were John's failings.

When we see our mate's problems, but don't see our own, it points to deep-rooted pride. The result is that we will focus our attention on our spouse rather than ourselves. But as we have already seen, you can't fix your spouse. The only person you can fix is yourself. How much better to expend your energy

Gospel Humility

fixing the one person you can fix—yourself—rather than the one person you can't fix—your spouse.

Humility pivots our attention from our spouse to self. The humble Christian has 20/20 clarity about their own sins and 20/500 about their spouse's. They focus their energy on fixing self.

This doesn't mean our spouse doesn't have real problems. It could be something serious like adultery, porn addiction, or total financial irresponsibility, etc. It doesn't mean their problems aren't worse than yours. It doesn't mean marriage counseling is a waste. Nor does it mean that you should just rollover and submit to abuse. A spouse should never put up with physical abuse, sexual abuse of children, drunkenness, drug addiction, porn addiction, or repeated adultery, etc. These need to be reported to your pastor, and when mandated by law, to the police. Rather, I am saying that the fundamental disposition of humility is to point the finger at the only person you can fix—self.

When both husband and wife are willing to do this, there is no marriage that cannot begin the journey back to Paradise.

Skilled marital counselors help couples through this transition by helping them own their own failings, while motivating them to run to the cross for forgiveness and encouragement.

I shared all of this with Janice, but she wasn't buying it. She refused to accept any responsibility. Instead, she responded indignantly, became agitated, left the room in anger, and refused all further efforts at counseling. A few months later she filed for divorce.

QUESTION 2—ARE YOU PATIENT OR IRRITABLE?

Impatience is one of my great sins. It is most likely to show up in my relationship with Judy. It is rarely her fault. Rather, it is the differences in our temperament that usually provoke it. I am type-A, and she is laid-back, go-with-the-flow, type-B. It is what I love about her, but when she doesn't bull her way ahead at my speed, I can become critical or impatient.

Impatience is an absence of love. Paul defines love in 1 Corinthians 13:4-7, and the first thing he says is, "Love is patient. Love is kind...It is not irritable or resentful"

Why is love patient and kind? Because love is humble. It looks up to others, and it values the diverse ways they process and do things. It doesn't look down on them because they are not just like me. True humility sees its weaknesses with great clarity, and that motivates compassion and *patience* with the weaknesses and differences of others. Humility feels how patient God has been with itself, and then shares that patience with its spouse.

Paul also says that "love...is not irritable" (Vs 5). Irritability is another symptom of pride. If you don't believe this, the next time you get irritable look inward. What is motivating you? Usually contempt. I am looking down on her because she is not like me. My spouse doesn't think like me. My spouse doesn't act like me. In fact, irritability is closely related to impatience. Most of us get irritable regularly. How much marital pain could be eliminated if we just learned to dissolve irritability in the solvent of humility? "In humility count others more significant than yourself" (Phil 2:3).

One day Judy and I walked into a Walmart, and I grabbed a shopping cart. Judy immediately pulled a disinfecting towel from the dispenser and begin to wipe down the cart handle. (Did I mention that she is very clean)? I rolled my eyes as if to say, *I can't believe you are doing this. It seems a little over the top, don't you think?* I was irritated.

But what was really going on? I thought my approach to the shopping cart was rational, and Judy's silly. I had elevated my opinion and way of doing things over hers. I was basically saying, *you need to be like me—a balanced, wholesome, down to earth person.* Behind all of this was an ugly assumption. I am superior. My way of thinking is superior. My outlook on life is superior. I have my life together, and you don't. You need to be like me.

I was not elevating the thoughts and opinions of my wife. I was not considering her approach "more important than mine." But this is how humility thinks. It looks up to and appreciates its mate. It watches her disinfecting the shopping cart handle and admires her, or at least accepts her differences non-condescendingly. Humility motivates us to place a high value on how our mate thinks and acts.

We learn patience and humility at the foot of the cross. What would happen if God was as impatient with our weaknesses, failings, and sins as we are with our spouse's? What would happen if he got irritable with us for the same petty reasons that cause us to get irritable? We would be incinerated on the spot. But we aren't. Why? In humility Jesus counted us more important than himself.

How do we cure impatience and irritability? When we stand at the foot of the cross we see Christ, absorbing the wrath that our impatience and irritability deserves. He does this so that God can be patient and gracious with each of us, who only deserve God's impatience and irritation.

Here is the simple truth. You will be patient with your mate to the degree that you feel God's patience toward yourself. You will feel God's patience toward yourself to the degree that you get in touch with your sins and what they deserve. This only happens in the shadow of the cross.

QUESTION 3—DO YOU SUSPECT SELF OR DEFEND SELF?

Believers growing in humility become increasingly suspicious of themselves. Even when they don't see it, they assume they are proud. They also assume they have an inflated view of their virtues. They assume they don't see self accurately, so even though none of us enjoy critique, they invite it. But hopefully when they do they don't respond like me.

One day my wife said, "Bill, can I share something with you?"

"Sure, what is it?"

"Promise you won't be mad at me?"

"Of course not. Why would I get mad?"

"At the party last night, you spoke critically about ____. You're the lead pastor. You set a bad example. People expect you to model what you preach. I know you didn't mean it, but your words hurt the cause of Christ."

"What do you mean 'critical speech?' I wasn't being critical. I was just making an important observation about ____. I shared it so we could help him grow."

What was I doing? I was not humbling myself and listening. I was justifying myself! My good opinion of self had been wounded, and I immediately unfurled the banner of self-defense. I became my own defense lawyer.

But people growing in humility have no delusions about themselves. They know they are sinners. The cross has already criticized them much more thoroughly than a spouse could ever do. There is Christ, receiving the punishment that my sins deserve, and I am humbled. The cross shatters my delusions of self-righteousness. It slams the door on my penchant for self-justification. That is why cross-centered Christians are most apt to advance in humility.

The cross motivates us to invite criticism and listen non-defensively. We want to be humbled. We want to grow in the knowledge of our imperfections so that we can change and descend deeper into the knowledge of the "unsearchable" riches of Christ.

This is not to say that all criticism is accurate. Sometimes it isn't. Sometimes bitterness, arrogance, or hurt motivates it.

When that is the case we need to listen cautiously. When the Devil spoke through Peter, Jesus responded, "Get behind me Satan" (Matthew 16:23). In the same way, the Devil may speak condemnation or ungodly criticism through your spouse or another. So, letting the truck of criticism role over you indiscriminately is not always appropriate. But when a spouse comes in gentleness, humility, and love we should listen attentively.

What does being suspicious of oneself look like? First, as we have already noted, it invites criticism. It wants to grow. Therefore, when the criticism comes, even when we may not fully see the sin in our self, humility responds something like this. "Thanks for the observation. I will pray about it." Then humility goes to God, "Father, if there is truth in my spouse's critique, let me see it."

Last, it runs to the cross for forgiveness and comfort. "Lord, you submitted to crucifixion because I can never measure up. You also died to forgive me and convince me that you will use my weaknesses for good. Thank you. Despite my failings, you still love me with an everlasting love."

So, God's critique of us at the cross does several things. It frees us to receive our mate's critique (always much less severe). Second, it reminds us that God will use our sins, failings, and weakness for good (Romans 8:28). Last, it lavishes us with forgiveness when we fail. This is how the gospel equips us to humble ourselves and hear a loving spouse's critique.

QUESTION 4—DO YOU DEMAND OR YIELD?

1 Corinthians 13 doesn't stop with impatience or irritability. It also adds, "Love does not insist on its own way" (1 Corinthians 13:5). In other words, it is not demanding. Rather, assuming it is not a compromise of God's will, humility finds great joy in yielding to its mate's desires and needs.

MARRIAGE IN PARADISE

In the car Judy prefers to listen to Pandora. I like podcasts about sports and current events. Who will yield? My wife prefers a plant-based diet. I like red meat, the more fat the better. Who will yield? Maybe you like to spend your vacation elk hunting or fishing in Alaska, but you wife would rather take the family to Disney Land. You want to spend your annual bonus on a new set of golf clubs, but your wife needs a new vacuum. Who will yield? Will you demand your rights or humbly walk in love? By reading this you can sense my conviction that it is the husband's job to set the example. Love means yielding wherever possible. It is her happiness at your expense.

When we refuse to let go of our demands—the vacation, podcast, or golf clubs—in biblical terms, they have become an idol. In fact, idolatry is the source of most fighting. Listen as James analyzes the source of our conflicts.

> What causes quarrels and what causes fights among you? Is it not this, that your passions are at war within you? You desire and do not have, so you murder. You covet and cannot obtain, so you fight and quarrel. You do not have, because you do not ask. You ask and do not receive, because you ask wrongly, to spend it on your passions. You adulterous people! Do you not know that friendship with the world is enmity with God? Therefore, whoever wishes to be a friend of the world makes himself an enemy of God (James 4:1–4).

Humble people want to be like Jesus. He considered us and our needs more important than his own (Philippians 2:3). 1 Corinthians 13 is a description of Christ. "Love...does not insist on its own way." In fact, he surrendered his rights. He left realms of glory, put the perks of divinity on the shelf, and took an *infinite* step down. He became a human being—a part of his creation. He became his Father's slave: "He humbled himself by becoming obedient to the point of death, even death on *a cross*" (Philippians 2:5-8).

The willingness to imitate Jesus is the road back to paradise. It is a road of gracious yielding.

CONCLUSION

This chapter has stressed the importance of humility. It is the antidote to pride, and pride is the heart and soul of Original Sin. Pride expresses itself as the idol of self. The idolatry of self is a marriage wrecking ball, destroying everything it touches. Humility is foundational to love, and love is the measure of our spiritual maturity. The most important person for you to love by humbling yourself is your spouse.

This chapter asked four questions by which to measure your humility, or its absence. Whose sin are you focused on? Are you patient or irritable? Are you suspicious of self or defending self? Are you demanding or yielding? The next chapter will deal with question five.

STUDY QUESTIONS

- Do you feel proud or humble? Be honest and tell the truth. What do these feelings say about your level of humility?
- How would you define humility? How would you define pride?
- Read Philippians 2:3-8. What do these verses tell us about the nature of true humility?
- Which of the four tests in this chapter am I best at? Which do I need the most improvement on? Why?
- On a scale of 1-10 ask your spouse to rate your humility. Ask why she or he give you that score? In light of this, what can you do to grow in humility?

NINE: Ambition?

THE LAST CHAPTER introduced the crucial subject of humility and pride. We learned that pride is foundational to Original Sin. We defined it as a pathological self-centeredness. We discovered that we all have this disease. Pride so inflates our view of self, that it blinds us to its very existence, and that is why proud people think they are humble.

By contrast God has opened the humble believer's spiritual eyes. He or she has a realistic view of self. This Christian sees both self and God realistically. They have 20/20 vision about their own sins and weaknesses and 20/500 about their spouse's, and the first sin the humble person begins to see is their pride. Therefore, the first mark of growing humility is the conviction that I am proud. The Christian growing in humility sees their pride and hates it. This Christian sees the connecting webs between pride and their other sins. They also increasingly elevate others, especially their spouse. Growth in humility is the first sign that a couple is on the road back to paradise.

Chapter eight suggested four questions to help us diagnose the level of our humility.
- Whose sin are you focused on?
- Do you struggle with impatience or irritability?
- Are you suspicious of self or defending self?
- Are you demanding or yielding?

Chapter nine will concern itself with question five.
- Is your ambition selfish or unselfish?

Chapter ten will complete our discussion by asking three final questions.

BRIAN AND HELEN

Brian is a contractor. He owns an excavation business. He works twelve-hour days, five days a week, sometimes more. He loves his work and is committed to growing his business.

He could work less, but he chooses not to. Why? Business is rewarding. Revenue growth strokes his ego. Besides life at home lacks the sizzle of the business world. His children are fussy. They cry, pout, need discipline, and demand attention. That is why he leaves at 7:00 AM, often not returning until 7:00 PM or later. By then the kids are in bed. The result? He rarely sees his wife and children. It is also why he spends two of his three weeks' vacation elk hunting with his buddies.

What drives Brian? Besides selfishness, he is insecure. His success is his identity. He wears it like a badge. When he enters the country club, he wants people to notice. He is ambitious, but for all the wrong things. He could be home for family meals but that would mean less success, and he is unwilling. He is building his ego at the expense of his wife and children.

His wife, Helen, is resentful. She has a three-year-old and a six-year-old. She feels like a full-time nanny. She loves mothering, but she is also starved for adult interaction. When she and Brian married they were deeply in love, but eight years later the excitement and the romance are gone. She feels unappreciated and devalued. She is jealous. Brian's business has become his mistress, and she is increasingly convinced that he loves it more than herself.

NATALIE AND TIM

Natalie grew up in a two-income home. Her mother was a professional. In addition, her college experience convinced her that it would be a moral failing to settle for anything less than a high-powered career. She needs a job for self-actualization. She has internalized the assumption that this could never come from motherhood alone.

Natalie's job leaves little energy for her three children aged 2, 4, and 7. She often picks them up at daycare and brings them home to fast food. When Natalie has the energy to prepare dinner, they eat after 7:00. In either case, there is little time for devotions or other family-rich activities.

Her husband, Tim, is a dentist. Financially, Natalie does not need to work. In fact, he regularly pleads with her to stay home. "When the kids get older you can go back to work." The children also plead with her to stay home.

But Natalie has no interest in settling for motherhood. What would her mother say? What would her friends say? Besides, she likes working. She is a skilled graphic designer; her boss and other employees praise her talent and comment on how much they need her. Why exchange this for dirty diapers and runny noses?

Natalie agrees that her family would benefit from her full-time presence, but she has justified her decision to work. After all, hadn't she learned from earliest memory that a woman's needs come first?

Natalie does not consider herself a feminist. Rather, she is an evangelical deeply involved at First Baptist Church. But, lurking in her subconscious is an assumption hostile to the gospel—one to which she has given little conscious thought. It would be a capitulation to patriarchal power structures to give up her career for husband and children. It would be as wrong for her husband to ask this as it would be for her to submit to his request.

QUESTION 5—IS YOUR AMBITION SELFISH OR UNSELFISH?

Ambition is either godly or diabolical depending upon whether the word "selfish" or "unselfish" precedes it. Selfish ambition, in either husband or wife, contradicts the gospel. Worse, it is a death blow to the life God intends his people to express. Our marriage will smell heavenly or hellish depending upon the nature of our ambition.

A long-standing tradition in the church, coupled with Jude 6, concurs that selfish ambition was the cause of Satan's fall. Many think Isaiah 14:13-15 describes it. Whether that is your conviction or not, this passage in Isaiah expresses the heart and soul of selfish ambition. Notice the five "I wills."
You [the prince of Babylon] said in your heart,

> *I will* ascend to heaven;
> above the stars of God
> *I will* set my throne on high;
> *I will* sit on the mount of assembly
> in the far reaches of the north;
> *I will* ascend above the heights of the clouds;
> *I will* make myself like the Most High.'
But you are brought down to Sheol,
> to the far reaches of the pit.

Selfish ambition is a great sin. Pride is its root and foundation. It thinks like this. *I will make myself great even if it comes at the expense of everyone around me.* In this passage Lucifer wanted to displace God.[1] God's response was swift and decisive. Everyone who exalts himself will be humbled. Lucifer was no exception. Verse 15 is God's judgment. "But you are brought down to Sheol, to the far reaches of the pit."

Contrast Satan's selfish ambition with Christ's incredible *unselfish* ambition. Christ did the exact opposite. He was ambitious, but for our flourishing at his expense. God's unselfish ambition saved us. With seventy-eight short English words, Philippians 2:5-8 (ESV), draws the most amazing picture of unselfish ambition. Lucifer exalted himself with five "I wills." By contrast, Jesus humbled himself with seven steps down.

> Though he was in the form of God, [he] did not count equality with God a thing to be grasped, but emptied himself, by taking the form of a servant (Gk. slave), being born in the likeness of men. And being found in human form, he humbled himself by becoming obedient to the point of death, even death on a cross.

Satan's ambition was totally selfish. Christ's ambition was utterly and completely *unselfish.* Satan's ambition was for his own glory at God's expense. Christ's ambition was for our glory at his expense. Christ's ambition was for the glory of God and the salvation of God's children, and the cross was his means to that end.

Which ambition drives you and me? Spiritually, it is a matter of life or death. Selfish ambition, in either husband or wife is a marriage wrecker. It is corrupting the marriages of Brian and Helen and Tim and Natalie. By contrast, unselfish ambition permeates the homes of the humble, and the joy of heaven is its wonderful fruit.

Selfish ambition tempted Natalie. Her job was not the issue. It was neither right nor wrong. It was a neutral issue. *Motives were the issue.* Would she lay down her ambitions for the good of her husband and children? Or, would she sacrifice their welfare to fulfill her ambitions?

Selfish ambition is the spiritual energy that drives gender feminism. It is important that we name it for what it is. It is important that we confess it's source. It is Satanic. In her excellent book, *The Essence of Feminism,* Kirsten Birket sums it up with great clarity.

> The liberation that feminism wants is the freedom to be the same as the most irresponsible of men. It is the freedom to be utterly self-centered and to sacrifice others for one's own convenience and comfort—the very accusation that feminists have thrown against men.[2]

From infancy, feminism has propagandized most Generation X and millennial females to believe that selfish ambition is a virtue. In their book, *Girls Uncovered,* gynecologists McIlhaney and Shuford, describe how this affects their patients.

> High school girls are ambitious. They expect to have a professional career. About one in four say they want a job that requires a doctoral degree, while another 40 percent say that they want to have a professional career, such as nursing or engineering, that does not require a doctoral-level degree. More girls than boys want to have a career as a professional. Only 1.6 percent of girls say they aspire to be a full-time homemaker.[3]

These ambitions are not bad in themselves. The problem is the assumption that the selfish pursuit of them is a virtue. Notice, there is no consideration of how these ambitions will affect future family commitments. The needs of husband and children are not part of the conversation. It is just assumed that they must not be allowed to get in the way of the woman's career needs.

Christians have no problem with women achieving and advancing. Women should have equal opportunity to succeed. But, with either husband or wife, selfish ambition is not pleasing to God. When career success comes at the expense of husband and children, Christians must resist with every fiber of their being.

The same is true for husbands. Think of Brian's situation. His career advance has also meant the neglect of wife and children; therefore, it also is sin.

Genesis 2 reminds us that God created Eve to be a helper. That means her ambition is to be for her husband's and children's success. In his excellent book, *Rescuing Ambition,* Dave Harvey writes—

> One great measure of our humility, is whether we can be ambitious for someone else's agenda. Not just tolerate and accommodate the goals of those over us, but adopt their vision, promote and pursue their dreams. Our willingness to make others a success is a great measure of the purity of our ambitions.[4]

This applies equally, but not in the same way, to husbands and wives. For example, a man's ambition for his wife's career success should not motivate him to become a a stay-at-home dad. That is because God did not create Adam to be Eve's helper—but the opposite. And Genesis 2, not contemporary culture, is our map for sex roles in marriage. The husband is the provider. His wife should marry him to help him succeed. She is his helpmate; he is not hers.

Theodore Roosevelt (1858-1919), the 26th President of the United States, struggled with selfish ambition. In 1898 the United States declared war on Spain. At the time Roosevelt was the assistant secretary of the Navy. Although married, and the father of six children, (one a new born and his oldest a teen struggling with depression), at age forty he abandoned his family for the fame, glory, and excitement of military adventure. He didn't need the money. He was independently wealthy. The army did not need Roosevelt. There were plenty of qualified men to serve.

Nevertheless, he unnecessarily took a commission in the Army, led a troop of cavalry up Cuba's San Juan Hill, repeatedly exposed himself to enemy fire, and eventually won the congressional medal of honor.[5]

Can you imagine the conversation that he must have had with his wife, Edith? "I'm going to join the army."

"You're going to do what? You're forty years old. You have six children at home. One is a new born. Your oldest son, Ted, is having mental problems. He is on the verge of a nervous breakdown. I need you at home. Your children need you. Please don't go. I don't want to be a widow."

"I know, but I've had this passion to experience combat for years. I am bored with the Navy. I need excitement, so I'm taking a commission in the Army. Don't worry. I'll up my life insurance."

This is what selfish ambition looks like. In either husband or wife, it is an ugly sin. It is a fruit of pride. It is the aroma of hell. It is the energy that motivates gender feminism, and in either husband or wife, it is the enemy of marriage in paradise.

The humility that the gospel produces is the exact opposite. It says, "It is your happiness at my expense." Where Roosevelt failed, Christian men and women look deeply into the divine nature revealed through the gospel and repent. They joyfully set aside their personal ambitions for the good of spouse and children.

Conclusion

God created Brian to be the provider. But God wanted him to do it for the sake of Christ and his family. When unselfish ambition is in the driver's seat, husbands make it a priority to get home for dinner. When possible, they cut back their hours, or they take a job that will let them spend more time at home.

Whether Natalie worked outside the home was not the issue. The issue was motives. Why was she working outside the home? In some situations, outside employment may be the most loving activity. It may be the best way to serve a husband and children.

My mother in law was an RN. When my wife was in grade school she worked part time to earn private school tuition for Judy and her siblings. A wife may need to work so that her husband can finish graduate school. She may work after her children leave home. The options are endless.

In each of these cases the husband and wife should carefully pray together. What is best for our family? What will most advance the gospel?

Again, the question is "why?" *Why am I doing this?* When the answer is selfish ambition, the gospel, and everything Christians profess to believe, is contradicted. Selfish ambition means my agenda at your expense. Selfish ambition is the fuel that powers hell. But unselfish ambition is the aroma of heaven. Its fruits are love, joy, and peace in the Holy Spirit.

We have three more questions to help us discern our level of humility. They are the subject of chapter ten.

MARRIAGE IN PARADISE

STUDY QUESTIONS
- What are some ways that selfish ambition drives men? Does your marriage or the marriage of an acquaintance suffer from it?
- Do you agree that selfish ambition is the root and foundation of feminism? Why or why not?
- Read Isaiah 14:13-15. Can you think of any characters in the Bible that express this sin?
- Read Philippians 2:5-11. What characteristics of unselfish ambition does this text display?
- Is selfish ambition an issue in your marriage? If so, how does God want you to respond?

TEN: Three Last Questions

A DISTANT RELATIVE, Blanche, died when I was in my teens. She was born in the eighteen seventies but lived well into her nineties. I lived with her the summer I was thirteen. Life with Blanche is not a pleasant memory; she was bitterness personified. She looked like she was perpetually sucking a lemon.

She married her husband, Will, in the eighteen nineties. Shortly after their marriage Will bought acreage in northwestern Montana, just south of the Canadian border and east of Glacier National Park. He tried to grow wheat. Everyone else knew better; they raised cattle. But Will was stubborn. The result was that twenty years later he had not made enough cash to replace the tar paper on their cabin. They had one surviving daughter, Lucille. She was born in the eighteen nineties.

Blanche gave birth to a second child, and that is where the trouble began. The winter was especially cold—temperatures below zero. Blanche wanted to put the baby in their bed. Instead Will put him in a cradle, in the hall, just outside the bedroom door. The baby caught a cold, probably RSV, and died. Only someone who has experienced this kind of tragedy can fully sympathize. The pain was excruciating. That winter Will and Blanche suffered greatly.

Part of their suffering was relational. Blanche never forgave Will. From that day forward, she shut down all intimate relations. It was her way of getting vengeance. That is why her daughter, Lucille, had no siblings.

Blanche had lived a difficult life. Her parents died when she was young. An unaffectionate aunt and uncle raised her. She had known nothing but hardship. Now this! If this poor woman had been a Christian, perhaps she would have had the resources to forgive, but she was not. Therefore, she had no reason to forgive. But for you and me, the motivations are different. We believe the gospel, and that is a game changer. This chapter will ask three final questions to test the level of our humility.

- Do you forgive aggressively?
- Do you speak to each other contemptuously?
- Are you grateful for your spouse or complaining?

QUESTION 6—DO YOU FORGIVE OR NURTURE RESENTMENT?

A marriage counselor once told me that, in his experience, bitterness destroys more marriages than any other sin. He was thinking about memories of deep hurts, stretching back decades, whose flame a spouse had deliberately nurtured. Another told me that, in her experience, most adultery was an attempt to get even with a spouse for unforgiven wounds never resolved and healed.

Not only does bitterness destroy marriages, it also destroys happiness. Blanche was one of the unhappiest people I have ever known. Why? It is impossible to nurse bitterness and be happy at the same time. Happy people forgive quickly. Unhappy people feed old grievances, justifying them, and refusing to let go.

Like selfish ambition, bitterness is a fruit of pride. Proud people feel that the sins and offenses of their spouse are so much greater than theirs, that they are entitled to be bitter.

By contrast, the further we descend the ladder of humility the quicker we joyfully forgive from the heart. The gospel humbles us, and that humility motivates us to forgive as Christ has forgiven us.

It is impossible to really understand and internalize the gospel and not be quick to forgive. Remember, humility is the ability to see myself with 20/20 clarity, and I get that insight while seated at the foot of the cross. What does the cross teach? What do I see there? I see God's Son taking the judgment that my sins deserve, and the judgment is brutal. Jesus absorbs the death penalty in my place. It wasn't a painless death by lethal injection. It was a slow, brutal death by horrendous torture.

That means I am guilty. My crime is capital. Because I deserve to be abandoned by God in hell forever, God abandons Jesus in my place. Jesus' death means my sins are so serious in God's sight that I deserve the unspeakable torments of the cross.

As we have seen, the cross simultaneously shows me the divine wrath that I deserve, and the amazing grace that I don't deserve. The cross reminds me that I am utterly unworthy of God's forgiveness, but absolutely loved by God anyway.

MARRIAGE IN PARADISE

Here is the amazing truth: Jesus went to extremes to forgive you and me of offenses much greater than any spouse could ever offend us. The cross says, *no one can sin against me like I have sinned against God.*

This is why forgiveness is such a grave issue. It is why God's forgiveness depends upon our willingness to forgive.

> For if you forgive others their trespasses, your heavenly Father will also forgive you, but if you do not forgive others their trespasses, neither will your Father forgive your trespasses (Matthew 6:14–15).[1]

Is Jesus saying that works (the willingness to forgive) are the ground of my salvation? No. Faith and faith alone saves, but saving faith believes the gospel. Therefore, my willingness to forgive is a litmus test of my faith in the gospel. Do I really understand and believe the gospel? Those who do, forgive earnestly and never quit.

I clearly remember when I first understood this. It was a few years after my conversion, and the realities of the cross were just starting to sink in. I was beginning to see what the cross said about my sin, and the question became painfully obvious. How could I ever deliberately nurse bitterness toward anyone? If God nursed bitterness like I do, I would spend eternity in Hell. If I didn't forgive, I would be the world's biggest hypocrite.

If all of this is true, why don't we forgive? We don't forgive because it is costly. It means releasing the right to retaliate. It means not demanding my pound of flesh. Here is how Andre Seu, columnist for *World Magazine,* describes the process.

> Forgiveness is a brutal mathematical transaction done with fully engaged faculties. It's my pain instead of yours. I eat the debt. I absorb the misery I wanted to dish out on you, and you go scot-free...It is wrought in private agony before it ever comes to public amnesty.[2]

My relative, Blanche, would not do this. Instead, she retaliated. The deep pain her husband, Will, unintentionally caused her she dished back in spades for decades.

Forgiveness is a discipline. Many reading this have been betrayed, used, or hurt in excruciating ways. For you, forgiveness is not a one and done process. It is a discipline. When Peter asked how many times we should forgive, Jesus responded, "seventy times seven" (Matthew 18:22). That means an infinite number of times. Each time the hurt returns, we forgive, and we never quit doing this until our life is swallowed up in Christ's eternal glory.

Forgiveness is not a feeling. It is a decision. You may still feel the hurt, but it's what you do with that hurt when it resurfaces that determines whether you are a forgiver or a person enslaved to bitterness. Remember, forgiveness is seventy times seven!

The test is greatest in marriage. No one can hurt you like your spouse. That is because you need no one's affection, esteem, encouragement, and acceptance like your spouse's. Marriage is the armory where the weapon of forgiveness is sharpened and polished to a fiery glow.

Do you forgive, or do you nurture resentment? For proud people forgiveness is a sign of weakness, but that is not how the humble see it. Forgiveness is a sign of great spiritual strength. It points to the presence of an all-pervasive divine life. It is the sweet aroma of the gospel. And, it will be our eternal inheritance in the world to come.

QUESTION 7— IS YOUR SPEECH HUMBLE OR PROUD?

In Matthew chapter twelve Jesus gave his disciples a profound insight, and it has everything to do with putting marriage on the road back to paradise.

> For out of the abundance of the heart the mouth speaks. The good person out of his good treasure brings forth good, and the

evil person out of his evil treasure brings forth evil. I tell you, on the day of judgment people will give account for every careless word they speak, for by your words you will be justified, and by your words you will be condemned (Matthew 12:34b–37).

We can sum it up this way. A proud heart speaks condescendingly and critically, but a humble heart speaks graciously. This is no small issue. More than anything else, the happiness of your marriage will rise or fall on *how you speak to your mate*. Consider the following—

Death and life [to your marriage] are in the power of the tongue, and those who love it will eat its fruits (Proverbs 18:21).

The lips of the righteous feed many [think spouse] (Proverbs 10:21).

A gentle tongue is a tree of life [to a marriage], but perverseness in it breaks the spirit (Proverbs 15:4).

From the fruit of his mouth a man [substitute marriage] is satisfied with good (Proverbs 12:14).

The tongue is a small member, yet it boasts of great things. How great a forest [i.e. marriage] is set ablaze by such a small fire" (James 3:5)!

John Gottman, a Jewish sociologist who specializes in marriage and teaches at the University of Washington in Seattle, has discovered that how we speak to each other is critical. In fact, his research indicates that how a couple speaks to each other is the number one predictor of divorce. He has, what he calls, a "love lab" in an apartment near Lake Washington. Couples volunteer to live there for several days. During their stay, Gottman records and studies their speech. In his New York Times best-selling book, *The Seven Principle for Making Marriage Work,* he claims that he can listen to a couple speak to each other for five minutes and predict with ninety one percent accuracy whether they will eventually divorce or stay married. What is the most pronounced verbal assassin of marriage? Contemptuous or condescending speech.

According to Gottman, fighting is not the problem. Couples in healthy marriages fight. The trouble occurs when our fighting degenerates into condescending or contemptuous speech. That is when permanent damage begins to occur.

Condescension and contempt are symptoms of arrogance. Of the two, contempt is the deadliest. Here is how Gottman defines it.

> Sarcasm and cynicism are types of contempt. So are name-calling, eye-rolling, sneering, mockery, and hostile humor. In whatever form, contempt...is poisonous to a relationship because it conveys disgust. It's virtually impossible to resolve a problem when your [spouse] is getting the message you're disgusted with him or her.[3]

Words of contempt point to a heart actively looking down on its mate, but looking down on another is the definition of arrogance. It says, "I am so much better than you that I can't believe you are doing, saying, or thinking that." Or, "If you were like me you would have it together, and we wouldn't be having this discussion." Need I say more? Could any attitude more fully repudiate the message of the gospel? In an article on divorce, Marc Theissen writes—

> When anger transforms into contempt, permanent damage takes place...A marriage can recover from anger. But when couples become contemptuous of each other, they will surely divorce.[4]

The converse is also true. Sociologists know that when a couple's positive statements to each other are twice as frequent as the negative it is very unlikely that they will ever divorce. But positive speech takes work. It is a discipline. It is not natural to us. It is learned behavior. It takes intentional practice for it to become an habitual way of life, a normal way of relating to each other.

A humble heart praises its spouse. Humble people look for evidences of grace in their spouse, then they put into words what they observe. Because the cross has critiqued them, they know what they deserve, and they are overwhelmed with gratitude. They take nothing good that their spouse does for granted, especially the little things.

"Thanks for making the bed this morning."

"It means so much that you took the time to refuel my car on the way home. You didn't have to do that. Thank you."

"You got a haircut today. I like it."

"I love that dress. It makes your eyes look blue."

"Did I ever tell you how much I appreciated that pasta dinner last night? Thank you."

"Thanks for working to support the family. I don't take that for granted. I thank God every day that you love me enough to provide for me. Thank you."

If you are not habitually doing this, it will not begin overnight. It is a discipline, a habitual way of looking at your spouse, and it comes from first looking at the cross.

If God spoke to us the way we speak to our mate, we would all perish for eternity. We deserve contempt and condescension. Why don't we receive it? Jesus went to the cross. On him God poured out all the contempt and condescension that we deserve. Jesus did this so that he and his Father could look to us without condescension, and welcome us into his family.

QUESTION 8—ARE YOU GRATEFUL OR COMPLAINING?

As just noted, a humble heart looks at the cross and sees what it deserves. It certainly doesn't deserve marriage, children, and a spouse that loves me, even though imperfectly. What it really deserves is eternal conscious torment. Therefore, even the most imperfect marriage motivates Christians living under the shadow of the cross to "abound with thanksgiving"

(Colossians 2:7). Millions of people will die having never been married, but if you are married, that won't be you, so be thankful.

Happy marriages cultivate the discipline of gratitude for each other. They work at it like a golf pro works at his swing. The social sciences agree. "After interviewing 468 married individuals on relationship satisfaction," notes Tim Challies, "covering everything from communication habits to finances, [researchers from the University of Georgia] found that the 'most consistent significant predictor' of happy marriages was whether one's spouse *expressed gratitude*."[5] That means more than thinking grateful thoughts. It means actually speaking them to your spouse regularly.

Here is the question. Are you grateful for your spouse? Maybe you are thinking, *Hold on Bill. You don't understand. How can I be grateful for someone who doesn't keep the house clean, or often works through the dinner hour, etc.?*

But the gospel is the basis for gratitude. It flows from the message of the cross. Even though you deserve crucifixion, by God's grace you have a spouse that is willing to live with you, raise children with you, and walk with you through loneliness, old age, and sickness.

For gospel-centered Christians, therefore, marriage is always a glass half full, not a glass half empty. When we put on our "gospel glasses" we look at our spouse and what do we see? Much better than we deserve. By contrast, pride sees a glass half empty. It thinks, *She doesn't measure up. I deserve much better.*

This was Rich and Cindy. To Rich, Cindy was never good enough, and she looked the part—down trodden, sad, and discouraged. Rich thought he deserved better, much better. Rich claimed to be a Christian. He claimed to believe the gospel, but all my attempts to help him apply the gospel to his marriage were unfruitful. The realities of the gospel never sank in. He never quit complaining about his wife. They eventually moved to Oklahoma, and I lost contact with them.

Can you thank God for your spouse? God is always at work in his or her life. Something good is happening. Can you see it, or does pride blind you? Humble people see God's grace at work in their spouse even during an argument. (But they usually wait for a better time and place to share it).

By contrast, pride doesn't see the good they do, only their weaknesses, failings, and shortcomings. It is not able to see God at work. Why? Like Rich, that person hasn't internalized the gospel. "I deserve better," it thinks. Because it is blind to its own sins and what it deserves, it can only complain. A proud heart is never satisfied. It always deserves better. A humble heart knows what it deserves, and therefore, every small evidence of grace in a mate is an event to celebrate with gratitude.

Gratitude is a big subject in Paul's letters. In fact, New Testament scholar P.T. Obrien notes that "Paul mentions the subject of thanksgiving in his letters more often, line for line, than any other Hellenistic author, pagan or Christian."[6] Paul's letters literally overflow with exhortations to live a grateful, thankful way of life. Because it is a big subject with Paul it should be a big subject with us also. That is why I wrote *The Secret of Spiritual Joy*— to help Christians grow in gratitude.

The cross had humbled Paul, and that is why he overflowed with gratitude. The same is true for every Christian spouse growing in humility. They practice the discipline of gratitude. No matter how deep their marital issues, a humble heart knows it deserves worse. It overflows with words of thanks. "Thanks for getting up and feeding the baby." "Thanks for marrying me. I don't deserve you." "Thanks for buying groceries today." "I am so thankful that you take the time to read the Bible to our children." The examples go on and on. C. J. Mahaney expresses it well.

An ungrateful person is a proud person. If I'm ungrateful, I'm arrogant. And if I'm arrogant, I need to remember God doesn't sympathize with me in that arrogance; He is opposed to the proud.[7]

Are you grateful for your marriage? Does your gratitude overflow in your speech? Every marriage returning to Paradise cultivates the discipline of gratitude.

GROWING IN HUMILITY

This chapter and the last two have asked eight questions to help you diagnose your level of humility. If you are like me, you probably feel conviction. You don't measure up. But be encouraged. I don't measure up either. This is the case for all believers. Because "You must be perfect as your heavenly Father is perfect" (Matthew 5:48) is the standard, we can never measure up. That is why we need a Savior.

So, the question remains. What can we do to grow in humility? It should already be apparent that cross-centered Christians are most apt to grow in humility. The cross affects us four ways.

First, the cross humbles us. As we have repeatedly seen, it shows us what we deserve. "Beholding God in his exalted majesty," observes Ray Ortlund, "and seeing ourselves in our sinful vileness, here in this moment of insight, humility—that is to say, realism—is reborn in our hearts."[8]

The cross confronts us with the awful reality of our sinfulness. We deserve nothing but crucifixion.

Second, not only does the cross show us what we deserve, it also portrays what God expects of us. Jesus is the picture, and it is one of humility. Jesus obeyed. His obedience was an act of humiliation. It said, "My only duty is obedience to the One who is infinitely greater." That is why Philippians reads, "He humbled himself *by becoming obedient*, even to the point of death, even death on a cross" (Philippians 2:8).

MARRIAGE IN PARADISE

Andrew Murray asks, "What was Christ's chief virtue?" Here is how he answers, "Humility. What is the incarnation but His heavenly humility...What is His life on earth but humility...And what is His atonement but humility? 'He humbled Himself and became obedient unto death'...Jesus of necessity was the Incarnate Humility."[9] This means that if we want to grow in humility we will need to carefully watch and imitate Jesus. He is humility incarnate.

Third, the grace of God demonstrated at the cross *motivates* humility. The more light the Holy Spirit sheds on the cross, the more Christ's moral beauty dazzles. At the heart of that beauty is humility. The natural response is worship, and we always *imitate* what we worship.

Last, the cross provides us with grace when we backslide into selfish pride, which, for most of us, is daily. Before writing this paragraph, I got into a fight with Judy over which of our cars, mine or hers, was best in the snow. Isn't that ridiculous? But that is what I am like, stubborn, petty, and proud. I thought I needed to be right, but that was not my real need. My real need was humility. My real need was God's grace. How about you?

Afterwards, when condemnation followed I fled to the cross. There was Jesus taking the wrath I deserve and crying "It [the wrath] is finished." God's grace encouraged me to keep trying despite repeated failure. As we have already noted, the cross convinces me that I am much more sinful than I ever imagined, even as it also convinces me that I am infinitely more loved than I ever imagined.

Here is the bottom line. We live in a Genesis 3 world. This means, even the best of us, wrestle daily with arrogance, and it will not cease until Christ liberates us in the purifying light of his ravishing presence (1 John 3:2). Only then will the pride of self be banished forever. Meanwhile, it is all out war, and even though we struggle, there is a huge difference between a believer fighting that war and sometimes losing a battle, and someone professing faith but unwilling to fight at all.

In summary, how does the cross affect us? It humbles us with the knowledge of our sin. It models what true humility looks like, then motivates us to imitate it. And last, it lavishes us with mercy, grace, and forgiveness when we fail.

In the words of the 18th century hymn writer, Isaac Watts.

"When I survey the wondrous cross

On which the Prince of Glory died

My richest gain I count but loss

And pour contempt on all my pride."

STUDY QUESTIONS

- Of the three symptoms of pride in this chapter—bitterness, condescending speech, and complaining—which do you have the biggest problem with? Why?
- Of the three symptoms of pride in this chapter, which do you have the least problem with and why?
- This chapter concluded with three ways the cross helps us pursue humility? Can you name them? Which is most relevant to you at this time in your life?
- How does God want you to respond to this chapter?

ELEVEN: Best Friends for Life

STAN AND KATE were in their mid-forties when they first sought counseling. After twenty years, their once happy marriage was in trouble. They were staring at an empty nest shared with a spouse that neither liked. Their oldest son, Michael, was a sophomore in college. Jim was a senior in high school, and Mary, their youngest, was a sophomore.

Deeply involved in their local church, their friends would have voted Stan and Kate least likely to need marriage counseling. They were spiritual pillars. A successful small group met in their home. Stan sat on the elder's board and owned a prospering small business. Kate was chairman of the high school booster club and deeply involved in a women's Bible study. They entertained constantly. In fact, their habitual outreach to new comers set an example for the other members of their growing church.

But over the last five years their relationship had slowly deteriorated. They had settled into the bottom of a relational pit. Neither wanted a divorce or separation, so here they were, in pastor Jim's office.

"Our marriage is in trouble," Stan began. "We didn't know where else to turn. We need help."

"It is hard to admit we have problems," Kate added. "Everyone thinks our marriage is together, but it isn't."

"Can you be more specific?" pastor Jim asked.

"We used to be best friends," Stan began, "but in the last five years, things have really gone downhill."

"We used to look for opportunities to be together," Kate added, "But now we do the opposite. It's just too painful. Our discussions always end in a fight. Last summer we actually vacationed separately. At first, I rationalized: this is temporary. We can fix it. Our relationship will get better. But it hasn't. It's getting worse."

"The kids are growing up," Stan added. "In five years they will be gone. Neither of us is looking forward to spending the rest of our life with someone we don't like. So here we are."

Pastor Jim picked up his clipboard and started asking some key diagnostic questions. "Do either of you practice regular personal devotions?"

"I used to," Stan answered with his eyes down. "I don't know what happened. I guess life got busy. I got distracted, and slowly I got out of the habit."

"How about you, Kate?"

"Same."

"I know it's something I should do," Stan continued, "and I feel guilty about it. The truth is, other things have become more important."

"Do you pray together?"

They gave each other a guilty look. "We used to," Stan answered. "When the kids were little we prayed together three or four times a week. But...I don't know...things got busy, and like my devotions, we've just slowly drifted from the habit."

"How long has it been?"

Stan looked at the floor, "Probably ten years."

"Do you read the Bible together?"

"Bible reading ended about the same time that prayer ended," Kate added.

"Why did you quit reading scripture together?"

"Probably the same reason we quit praying together." Stan said. "It was never a deliberate decision. We just quit...I don't know. Life got hectic: it just wasn't a priority. The kids got into soccer. Their activities began to fill up our evenings. Mary got into gymnastics. Jim, our middle boy, joined the chess club, and Michael had his college activities. Kate became a full-time taxi driver. I was working long hours building my business."

"Do you take time to talk about what God is doing in your lives?"

"I do that in my men's Bible study," Stan answered, "but I never thought about doing it with Kate, especially in light of our fighting."

"Same here," Kate added. "I share with my girlfriends. I'd like to with Stan, but I am afraid to even try."

"How about dates?" pastor Jim asked. "Do you go on dates together? Do you ever go out of town, just the two of you, overnight for a romantic weekend?"

"We used to," Stan said. "Then the kids came," Kate added. "Things got crazy-busy. I think we just assumed we didn't need that anymore. The kids were little. Babysitters were hard to come by, and they were expensive. We gave up without even talking about it."

Stan and Kate were in the middle of a common marital problem. They had quit being best friends. This matters because friendship is the foundation for true love.

GOSPEL FRIENDSHIP

Chapter four, Paradise Restored, discussed God's plan for marriage as Paul described it in Ephesians five. We learned that God created human marriage to glorify Christ's marriage to his church. Christ is so intimate with his bride that the Bible describes them as one flesh (John 17). The Spirit of the Groom actually indwells each member of his bride communicating love, forgiveness, and fullness. This means that a husband and wife in a boring, or worse, hostile relationship, are not making the relationship between Christ and his bride look good. Just the opposite. This is a problem because making the romance between Christ and his bride look good is the purpose for marriage.

This was Stan and Kate. How many reading this are in a comparable situation? Deeply in love on their wedding day, they sought opportunities to be alone. They loved to be together. But the years passed and slowly, imperceptibly, their relationship changed. One day they woke up to the reality that their once vibrant intimacy had morphed into open hostility. Two best friends had become mere roommates, or worse, enemies.

Stan and Kate's story contains an important lesson. Relational intimacy is not automatic. It doesn't just happen. It requires intentionality. *We never drift towards anything good.* That includes marriage relationships. Spousal friendship takes effort. Wise couples make the effort, and they do it for several reasons. First, they believe it matters to God, and second, they also believe that God richly rewards those who seek him (Hebrews 11:6), and befriending your spouse is one important way to seek God. The couple that gives up on, or ignores, relational intimacy, ends up with a boring, plodding relationship, or worse, open hostility. A marriage like this does not glorify God, and to a man and wife caught in this trap, the thought of continuing sometimes seems hopeless.

By contrast, the road back to paradise is paved with an ever deepening, vibrant, friendship. Best friends love to be alone. They don't need to double date. They don't fear their children growing up and leaving home. They don't take separate vacations. They like each other. There is no one with whom they would rather spend a day.

Even secular social scientists have discovered the importance of "marital friendship." We already mentioned sociologist, John Gottman. He runs the University of Washington "love lab" to answer this question: what is the fundamental ingredient that every successful marriage shares? Here is what he discovered.

> Happy marriages, are based on a deep friendship. By this I mean a mutual respect for and enjoyment of each other's company. These couples tend to know each other intimately—they are well versed in each other's likes, dislikes, personality quirks, hopes, and dreams.[1]

Gottman stresses that this doesn't mean the absence of fights, stress, or relational issues. Marriages can fight volcanically and still be very happy. That is because the underlying friendship equips the couple to repair the damage and move on. According to Gottman, a robust marital friendship will solve many lesser problems—problems that would derail another marriage.

Because we are Christians we possess a powerful incentive for spousal friendship that Gottman lacks—the gospel. As we have seen, Christians pursue friendship in marriage to make the relationship between Christ and his bride, created by the gospel, look good.

So, what is the secret to marital friendship? The secret is a methodical, disciplined approach to our relationship with God, and a methodical, disciplined approach to our relationship with each other, in that order.

We don't usually associate the words methodical and discipline with friendship. Many have bought the lie that intimacy should be spontaneous. If not, we reason, it isn't "authentic." Sometimes intimacy is spontaneous, but the wise couple also practices the *discipline* of friendship, and this is the marriage that usually reaps the long-term fruit. Stan and Kate had been neither methodical, nor disciplined, and they were reaping the results. The foundation for spousal friendship starts with a vital and living relationship with God.

VERTICAL DISCIPLINES

Before a couple comes to me for marriage counseling I give them a questionnaire. I ask them to complete it without comparing their answers to each other. After I get it back, I schedule our first appointment. It contains questions like, who is the spiritual leader in your relationship? Do you consistently practice personal devotions? Do you pray together? Do you read the Bible together? Do you go on date nights? Do you ever leave your children overnight to be alone? For example, I have never encountered a troubled marriage where the husband and wife regularly prayed or read the Bible together. I'm not saying it never happens: I am saying that it's rare. I'm saying that it's never happened to me.

Of course, the question follows—did they quit praying together because of stress in their marriage, or was their failure to pray together the cause of their marital stress? In either case, in my experience, alienated couples rarely pray together, or practice the other spiritual disciplines either. That is because *the closer a couple gets to God, the closer they inevitably get to each other*. Figure 3 illustrates this principle. The opposite is also true. The further they go down the line, away from God, the further they get from each other.

Best Friends For Life

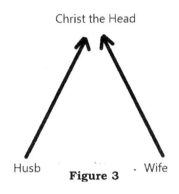

Figure 3

In other words, intimacy with Christ and intimacy with each other are seldom separated. "I am deeply convinced from Scripture, my own experience, and the stories of others," writes Paul Tripp, "that you fix a marriage vertically before you ever fix it horizontally."[2] For this reason wise counselors fix most broken marriages by starting where you would least expect, not with each other, but with the vertical—their relationship with Christ.

How do we build our vertical relationship? It's not rocket science. We build it through personal devotions, church attendance, praying and reading the Bible together.

When Pastor Jim asked Stan and Kate about their personal devotions he heard what he expected. They didn't pray together. In addition, for many years they had both fallen out of the daily habit of personal devotions. Their first assignment, therefore, was for them to schedule, and be faithful to, personal devotions for at least thirty minutes a day five day per week. He gave them texts to meditate on. They agreed to follow up in two weeks.

Attending church together is also a crucial spiritual discipline. That is because the local church is the most significant long-term influence on most people's spiritual maturation. This they were doing, and the pastor praised them for it, but mutual church attendance is not always the case.

In the rare cases when they don't attend the same church, the counselor should ask why? Attending the same church *together* is crucial. The important principle is that the husband accepts his responsibility to select a church for his family. Of course, a loving husband will solicit and carefully listen to his wife's input, but ultimately it is his call, and it is God's will that his wife be willing to support and follow him. The most important thing for him to look for is sound theology expressed through effective preaching.

After they had established a track record of personal devotions pastor Jim added step two. He assigned them the task of reading the Bible and praying together for at least fifteen minutes a day. They agreed to meet again in two weeks.

The Devil does not want you praying or reading the Bible together. Like many couples Judy and I struggled to pray together. Within eighteen months of our marriage we were both converted, but it was ten years before we started regularly praying together. Why? The first answer is my sinful laziness. The second was demonic resistance. Sometimes Judy would yawn during our attempts to pray together, and I would get irritated. I'm sure she felt the same about me. Couples that establish the discipline of prayer together push through resistance.

It doesn't need to be long. Fifteen minutes of Bible reading and prayer is sufficient. Nevertheless, it took some serious repenting on my part to launch a consistent mutual devotional time together.

This is primarily the husband's responsibility. Biblical masculinity is not about big muscles and macho. Biblical masculinity is about initiating in spiritual things. Ephesians five commands husbands to "wash their wives with the word." This does not mean standing behind a living room pulpit and preaching to an audience of one (or more if your children are still at home). It means a willingness to focus your marriage and family around God through his Word.

What did this look like for us? When our children were still at home it meant family devotions. After dinner, after the table was cleared, I would open the Bible to a paragraph or chapter. Then I would ask Judy or one of children to read it. The next five to ten minutes were discussion. I would ask questions. "What is this text about? What is God telling us? What surprises you about this passage? What claim does this text make on your life?" We would then close with a few minutes of prayer.

If you have a better idea or practice, I am all ears. The important thing is that the husband assumes responsibility for this practice, and second, that the practice centers his family on God through his Word.

Even though our children are now married and have their own families, Judy and I still follow this routine. It isn't always fun or exciting. Fireworks don't usually go off, but there is no practice more important, long term, to the quality of your marriage and family experience.

Back to Stan and Kate. Two weeks later pastor Jim met them. They were making progress. It was two steps forward, and one step back, but they were willing to try and make the changes pastor Jim recommended. It showed in their body language. They were actually holding hands!

CONCLUSION

A robust friendship is the heart and soul of a good marriage. A healthy growing friendship between a husband and wife points everyone to the healthy relationship between Christ and his bride, the church. A couple tired of each other, or worse, at war with each other, says *Christ and his bride have lost interest in each other*. And of course, nothing could be further from the truth.

Marital friendship happens to those who *intentionally* and *methodically* pursue it. It is work, but God richly rewards the labor. The first step is vertical. Focus on your relationship with Christ. Build it, and good things will happen. Inculcate the disciplines of daily devotions, church attendance, family prayer and Bible reading.

The second step is horizontal, and that is the subject of the next chapter.

STUDY QUESTIONS

- On a scale of 1-10, how would you rate the depth of your friendship with your spouse? Why that number? Why not higher?
- Do you agree that your relationship with your spouse will be according to your relationship with Christ? Is this formula too simplistic? Why or why not?
- On a scale of 1-10 how would you rate your devotional life? Why that number?
- In your opinion, why is it so hard to be consistent with daily devotions?
- What obstacles do you face when trying to establish a time to pray and read scripture together?
- Do you agree that it is the husband's responsibility to initiate Bible reading and prayer with his family? Why?

TWELVE: Building on the Foundation

IN THE LAST CHAPTER WE LEARNED THAT the foundation for a healthy marital friendship is a deeper relationship with God. Stan and Kate began to repair that foundation, and then they began to build on it. They focused their attention on their horizontal relationship.

In answer to pastor Jim's questions they confessed that they were not intentionally spending time alone together. They were not going on dates. They were not sharing with each other what God was doing in their lives. They were not practicing routine kindness to each other.

Friendship is the root that nourishes the tree of romance. In my early twenties, when Judy and I were still dating, my father gave me this excellent advice. "Marry your best friend." I remember thinking, *What does being a best friend have to do with romance, sex, and marriage? What happened to passion and love? Best friends? Boring!* However, forty-seven years of marriage have confirmed my father's wisdom. True love—the really passionate kind that everyone wants—is based on a deep, abiding, and vibrant friendship. Like our relationship with God, this relationship is not automatic. It doesn't mechanically take place because you and your spouse sleep in the same bed and share children. Spouses that are "best friends" are best friends because they work at it!

The church has not always considered marital friendship a priority. For example, Thomas Aquinas, a medieval Catholic theologian, wrote, "In all respects, a man will always make [another man] a better companion and helpmate than a woman."[1] Aquinas, a heterosexual single man, and a student of Aristotle, was merely reflecting the attitudes of the Greek philosopher that he so greatly admired. He also summed up the prevailing medieval European attitude toward marriage.

However, because it was a recovery of the Bible, the 16th century Reformation changed all of this. We have already noted Luther's marriage to Katie Von Bora. Martin and Katie were best friends. About marriage he famously wrote. "There is no more lovely, friendly or charming relationship, communion or company, than a good marriage." Luther's marriage presented a powerful new model—spouses as best friends—and Ephesians five was its rationale.

The Luthers had a wonderful friendship because they worked at it. In his book, *Luther on the Christian Life,* Carl Trueman describes how

> Today, visitors to the Augustinian cloister in Wittenberg (a gift from the elector to the Luthers on their wedding day) will see that the door frame has a little stool built into it on each side. The door frame was a present from Katie to her husband, made

at a time when she felt they were not spending enough time talking to each other. Thus, at the end of a busy day, Martin and Katie could sit on either side of the door and talk to each other. Inside and upstairs, there is a window frame with a similar arrangement, presumably for when the Saxon weather made an outdoor conversation wet and cold. This by itself speaks eloquently of the love and the happiness that marriage brought to the life of the Reformer.[2]

The moral is simple. Do whatever you must to build a friendship with your spouse, even if it means seats in your door frames.

This biblical ideal culminated with the 17th century English Puritans. Because Puritanism was the high-water of the Reformation, it was also the high-water of the biblical marital model. I quoted the Puritan pastor, Thomas Gataker, in the first chapter. He spoke for many when he wrote of his own marriage,

> There is no society more near, more entire, more needful, more kindly, more delightful, more comfortable, more constant, more continual, than the society of man and wife, the main root, source, and original of all other societies.[3]

The New Testament expectation for marriage is utterly unique. Contrast it with the marital ideal of Islam, Hinduism, or Shintoism. These religions would all be more comfortable with the medieval view of Aquinas.

Shintoism is the main religion in Japan. My daughter and her husband were missionaries there for four years. They befriended many Japanese couples. They learned that the Japanese rarely expected friendship or romance in marriage. It was purely functional. It was about children and family connections. Many husbands left Monday morning for work and didn't come home until late Friday night. There was little expectation of marital fidelity, let alone intimacy or a deep and abiding friendship.

Friendship is also assumed by the modern secular view of marriage, but for entirely different reasons. F. Bradford Wilcox, a nationally noted expert on marriage, describes the contemporary model this way—

> Increasingly, marriage [is] seen as a vehicle for a self-oriented ethic of romance, intimacy, and fulfillment. In this new psychological approach to married life, one's primary obligation [is] not to one's family *but to one's self;* hence, marital success [is] defined not by successfully meeting obligations to one's spouse and children but by *a strong sense of subjective happiness in marriage* — usually to be found in and through an intense, emotional relationship with one's spouse. The 1970s marked the period when, for many Americans, a more institutional model of marriage gave way to [this] 'soul-mate model.'[4]

This secular model, described by Bradford, is the Christian ideal gone to seed. We and our unbelieving friends share a common marital goal, friendship (intimacy), but with completely different means and for completely different ends. The end of Christian marital friendship is the glory of God. The means to that end include serving and/or inconvenience. The non-Christian's goal is simply personal peace and self-actualization. The means to that end is "you serve me." The means for the Christian is "I will lay down my life for you." A worldview Grand Canyon separates these perspectives.

Here is the fatal flaw in the secular model: as long as our only obligation in marriage "is to self," the marital friendship (or intimacy) pursued will constantly elude us. Christians pursue friendship by dying to it, by sacrificing self for the good of their spouse. They look beyond their relationship to the Lord. Their marriage is not ultimate. God is. Their expectations are realistic. They know they are not perfect, their spouse is not perfect, and that they are both sinners living in a fallen world.

Christian marital friendship thrives on acts of self-sacrifice. "When the Bible speaks of love," notes Tim Keller, "it measures it primarily not by how much you want to receive but by how much you are willing to *give of yourself* to someone. How much are you *willing to lose* for the sake of this person? How much of your freedom are you *willing to forsake?* How much of your precious time, emotion, and resources are you willing to invest?"[5]

What can a Christian couple reading this do to deepen their friendship? In this chapter I will stress shared goals, mutual respect, acts of kindness, intentionally scheduling time alone together, and the regular practice of biblical fellowship. We will take these one at a time.

SHARED GOALS

Stan and Kate (mentioned in the last chapter) shared the same goals, but they were not pursuing them together. However, many couples don't share the same goals. Sometimes, it is because they have never discussed their goals. At other times the problem is a lack of submission to God's goals for our marriage. Sometimes it is just a collision between the way men and women relate.

In his books on boys, girls, and gender, Dr. Leonard Sax discusses the different ways boys and girls experience friendships.[6] Boys experience what he calls, "shoulder to shoulder" friendship. Their relationship is a byproduct of a mutual interest in something else—hunting, football, politics, or their work. By contrast girls, relate "face to face." For them the relationship is the main thing. The friendship exists for its own sake.

Each approach has strengths and weaknesses. "Face to face" is why so many teenage girls are in constant relational turmoil. The relationship has become an idol. Shoulder to shoulder is why so many men have difficulty being transparent and sharing their feelings. Making the friendship obsessive is the danger for women. An unwillingness to talk about feelings is the danger for men.

Obviously, these are generalizations. There are many exceptions, but the fact that they are exceptions proves the truth of the generalization.

Healthy marital friendships share the best of both models. First, they relate shoulder to shoulder. The basis of their friendship—what unites husband and wife—are common goals for their marriage, common goals for their children, common goals for life after children, common goals for eternity, and how to help each other get there.

But, they also relate face to face. Both husband and wife are able and willing to be transparent and vulnerable. For both this requires dying to self. We will discuss face to face later, but since this section is about shared goals we will focus on shoulder to shoulder.

There is a minimum of three shared goals. First, a Christian husband and wife should obviously share a common commitment to Christ and his Kingdom. In biblical terms, they must be "equally yoked." "Do not be unequally yoked with unbelievers. For what partnership has righteousness with lawlessness? Or what fellowship has light with darkness" (2 Corinthians 6:14)? The biblical image is two oxen yoked together, side by side, pulling the same load, in the same direction, toward the same destination. "Equally yoked" implies oneness of vision and purpose.

This means a mutual decision to daily surrender to the lordship of Christ. "Lordship" means Christ is my boss. He runs my life. I do what he wants, not what I want. No matter the cost, I will follow him. "Lordship" implies authority. It means checking my rights and freedoms at the door as I enter God's kingdom. Obviously, I can't share this goal with an unbeliever. I must be married to a fellow Christian.

Many couples marry, and later one becomes a believer. This obviously means a lack of shared goals, and a friendship that will not go as deep as it could. Nevertheless, the believer has taken a vow that he or she will be faithful until parted by death. This means that every effort to build a rewarding friendship, despite the absence of this crucial shared purpose, matters to God.

Not only do healthy marital friendships thrive on a shared submission to the lordship of Christ, but they also thrive on shared goals for marriage and family. That means a commitment to biblical men and women's roles in marriage as discussed in previous chapters. It means a willingness to prioritize the husband's calling (Genesis 2:18), a mutual commitment to, and understanding of what well-disciplined and instructed children look like (Ephesians 6:4), [7] and a resolve to help each other persevere in the obedience of faith to the end of life.

Of course, we could mention many other shared goals, but these are the essentials. A Christian couple will not enjoy the friendship that God intends without a shared commitment to at least these.

RESPECT

Respect is a second crucial foundation for marital friendship. Stan and Kate were doing this well. They didn't like each other, but they did respect each other. However, this is not always the case.

In their second year of marriage Kim and John signed on with a missionary agency in Papua New Guinea. They rented a brick one-bedroom home in an area where earthquakes regularly occurred. Should they feel an earthquake they were advised to get out immediately.

One day, the building began to shake, the ground began to roll, and ceiling mortar began to fall. John and Kim headed for the door and arrived simultaneously. In a moment of panic, John pushed Kim out of the way and ran through ahead of her.

Fifteen years later they were in marriage counseling. After some diagnostic questions Kim mentioned that she did not respect John. When I asked why, she related the earthquake story. She knew that biblical masculinity is a willingness to unselfishly protect and serve women and children. John didn't do this. Instead, he protected himself at her expense, and she had never gotten over it. He had forfeited her respect.

Scripture gives us two reasons to respect someone. The first is their position. This God commands, whether the person has earned it or not. Paul concludes Ephesians 5. "And see that the wife *respects* her husband" (Vs. 33). She is to respect the position that God has given him. He is the head of her home. Although this kind of respect keeps order in the home, more is required for a deep and abiding friendship.

The respect that friendship rests on is *earned*. It is respect for someone's moral character. John's behavior during the earthquake forfeited Kim's respect. Had he stepped aside and pushed her through the door first, he would have earned her respect.

In addition to moral failure, we forfeit respect when we fear our spouse's disapproval more than we fear God's. In biblical terms, the spouse has become an idol. Husbands and wives in healthy relationships have convinced each other that God's approval matters more than each other's.

A friend and his wife were both raised Roman Catholic. Shortly after their conversion he realized that staying in the Catholic Church was not an option. She could sense this, and it made her anxious. Very close to her parents, she knew leaving the Catholic Church would devastate them and her extended family.

Building On the Foundation

Therefore, the husband feared that this decision would mean her disapproval and conflict. He had no idea how she would react. They were newly married. Would she divorce him? Would she separate? He didn't know. He was fearful. God was testing him.

Nevertheless, walking home one night from a prayer meeting, he shared his decision. She became so angry that all the way home she walked twenty paces behind him. Eventually, she warmed up to the idea, and followed him to a Protestant church. It all came down to this: his willingness to make God more important than his spouse. It is fundamental to a healthy and abiding friendship.

A woman's husband asked her to sign their annual tax return. She knew he had lied about their income. "I can't sign it until you correct the dishonesties," she said. He was furious, but she was adamant. She feared God's disapproval more than his.

This kind of relational idolatry was part of Adam's temptation. Eve was an amazing gift. Imagine how happy he and Eve were in a sinless environment? Therefore, the Serpent tempted him to love the gift more than the Giver.

Did the Devil tempt Eve, not Adam, because he knew that fear of Eve's disapproval would be Adam's great test? After she ate the forbidden fruit the text reads. She "gave some to her husband who was with her, and he ate" (Genesis 3:6b).

Two facts stand out. First, Adam was with her. He witnessed the entire dialogue with the Serpent and did not intervene. Second, he feared Eve's disapproval more than he feared God's. When she offered him the fruit he should have said, "Eve, I can't. You know God's command. I fear his disapproval more than yours. I would rather incur your rejection than God's." But, he didn't.

The rest is history.

MARRIAGE IN PARADISE

Our ability to enjoy any relationship is according to our willingness to make God more important. Here is how the always quotable C. S. Lewis put it.

> Every preference of a small good to a great, or partial good to a total good, involves the loss of the small or partial good for which the sacrifice is made...You can't get second things by putting them first. You get second things only by putting first things first.[8]

In his book, *What Did You Expect?* Paul Tripp makes the same point.

> You and I will never understand our marriages and never be satisfied with them until we understand that marriage is not an end to itself. No, the reality is that marriage has been designed by God to be a means to an end.[9]

The "end" Tripp has in mind is God. Marital friendship thrives when we put God first and our spouse second. Fearing the disapproval of God more than our mate's, although it might cause immediate conflict, is the foundation for long-term relational intimacy.

> If anyone comes to me and does not hate his own father and mother and *wife* and children and brothers and sisters, yes, and even his own life, he cannot be my disciple" (Luke 14:26).

> "And he said to them, "Truly, I say to you, there is no one who has left house or *wife* or brothers or parents or children, for the sake of the kingdom of God, who will not receive many times more in this time, and in the age to come eternal life (Luke 18:29–30).

In summary, marital friendship is built on shared life goals, but it also requires *earned* respect. It is difficult, if not impossible, to go very deep in friendship, let alone intimacy, with someone who has not earned your respect.

If you are single, don't even consider marrying someone you don't respect this way.

ACTS OF KINDNESS AND SERVICE

In the heat of their pain Stan and Kate had almost completely quit serving each other with small acts of kindness. Instead, they intentionally avoided each other.

However, routine acts of kindness are the third foundation for marital friendship. They say, "I love you. I value you. You are special to me." I don't mean *random* acts of kindness. I mean premeditated, carefully thought out, routine acts of kindness.

Ted and Margie are a good example. They study each other so that they can serve each other. That is what friends do. Margie has allergies, and flowers set them off. She is also allergic to most perfumes. On the other hand, she loves to buy clothes and she loves to watch movies on the big screen.

So, Ted doesn't give her flowers or perfume. He takes her to a movie she has been wanting to see. For Christmas he buys her a gift certificate to a local clothing boutique. Margie likes to have him tag along. She wants his opinion, so he takes the sports page and reads while she tries on outfits. This is what friends do. Yes, Ted feels a bit awkward in a women's clothing store. He doesn't get how Margie can try on outfit after outfit and find nothing she likes. But he loves his wife, and this is how he shows it. It's the kind of thing friends do.

Sometimes, even though he would rather do something else, he watches a romantic comedy with her. When she gets depressed, he takes her out to dinner. When she needs time alone, he gives her his debit card and sends her to Starbucks for a few hours. On Saturday morning Ted makes blueberry pancakes for the family, but because Margie doesn't like blue berries, he takes hers out.

Margie studies Ted the same way. He needs fifteen minutes re-entry time on arrival from work, so she and the children leave him alone. Ted likes drumsticks, so when Margie makes fried chicken he gets them both. Margie is a great gifter. She doesn't gift what she would like. Instead, she studies Ted and gives him the special gift she knows he has been wanting.

Best friends watch and study each other. They understand the importance of small acts of kindness. Some even keep a journal so they can remember what their spouse likes and doesn't. In all the little areas they practice acts of kindness. That is what friends do, and acts of service and kindness like these deeply enrich marital friendship.

TIME ALONE

When we were out of town, our sprinkler system broke down, and a substantial portion of our lawn died. Lawns don't grow naturally. They require three things: sun, water, and food. So, I very intentionally went about methodically giving my lawn the two latter ingredients. (God graciously provided the sun). I fixed the sprinkler system and consistently applied fertilizer. Over a two-month period it gradually came back. Marital friendship works the same way. It doesn't just happen. It requires intentionality.

Friendship thrives on unhurried, scheduled time alone together. That is the fourth ingredient. When couples don't like each other time alone is an act of faith. Stan and Kate didn't like each other. They had long ago quit spending time alone, and it showed, but they were willing to try.

When a relationship has degenerated to this extent it needs a plan, and the plan needs to be applied. "Get your schedules out weekly," pastor Jim told them, "and put a time on your calendar. This is your assignment for the next two weeks." They did, and their friendship is slowly putting down roots and growing upward.

A thriving marital friendship presupposes that your children come second. There are at least three reasons to make them second. First, it will make them happy. There is an old saying, the most important thing a couple can do for their children is to love each other. When children see dad and mom delighting in each other, they feel happy and secure. In addition, they will grow up and make their own marriages a priority.

The second reason to prioritize your relationship is long term. Most couples will be together fifty years or more. That means you will spend many decades as empty nesters. When Judy and I do marriage conferences we always remind those listening that most modern marriages will enjoy more years without children than with them. For these last decades to glorify God you must make your relationship a priority from the earliest years.

Therefore, don't build your marriage around your children. Build it around God, then each other, then lastly your children. They will be here today and gone tomorrow, but you and your spouse are together until parted by death. That's a long time. We had children under our roof from 1973 to 2000, 27 years. Since that time, we have been childless. At this writing we have not had children in our home for 18 years. Because we prioritized our friendship, the childless years have been richly rewarding.

Besides making your children secure, and the reality that you will spend many childless years together, there is a third reason to prioritize your relationship. It is God's will. Think about it. You will never be "one flesh" with your children, but you are with your spouse. Your relationship with your children will never glorify Christ's marriage to his church, but your marriage will. So, prioritize your marriage. Spend time alone away from your children.

Couples that successfully carve out time alone are creative. Maybe you don't have enough money to go out. Put the children to bed and do a candlelight dinner at home. Barbecue your favorite steak or seafood. Add a bottle of wine, light the candles, and put on some background music. Make it special.

For those who can afford it, get a babysitter. Maybe you'd rather go to the park and talk while you walk. Some go rock climbing, others to a movie. I know one couple that likes to drive through a nice part of town looking at houses. If you can afford it go out to dinner, and afterwards sit on a bench and watch the sun go down.

Friendships also thrive on the routine celebration of important milestones. One of my pastor friends calls it "Hotel Time." When our kids were in junior high and older we started going away for a few days every year on our anniversary (in June). When our children were in high school and college we added a second weekend in November—the anniversary of our first date. So, every six months we go away together alone. Time alone is one key to a healthy, vibrant friendship.

BIBLICAL FELLOWSHIP

A fourth foundation for marital friendship is "fellowship." Fellowship is a New Testament word. It translates the Greek word, koinonia. Sometimes it gets translated communion, at other times participation, or partnership. In his book, *Eighteen Words,* J. I. Packer defines it as "sharing with our fellow-believers the things that God has made known to us about Himself and listening to them share the same with our self."[10]

Our church meets in small groups to practice this kind of fellowship. Sometimes I ask, "How many of you practice this fellowship in your marriage?" Usually, very few hands go up. This is a bad sign. Why? Because spiritual friendship thrives on biblical fellowship.

As we have seen, women tend to relate face to face. Intimacy means talking about feelings. This is what women want and, therefore men, it's what we need to give. "Husbands, love your wives as Christ loved his church and gave himself up for her." Nothing opens the inner recesses of who we really are like talking about our relationship with God, our successes and failures, and how we feel about them.

Even though this is unnatural for many men, it is the husband's responsibility to initiate it. That's what masculinity does. It initiates. "What has God been saying to you lately? What has God been teaching you from his word? Have you experienced any conviction of sin lately? Where has God recently encouraged you?" He should reciprocate by answering the questions he is asking.

Fellowship implies transparency, including the confession of sin. "Confess your sins to one another and pray for one another" (James 5:16). For some this is easy with everyone but their spouse. Nevertheless, a test of marital friendship is the willingness to relate this way. Stan and Kate's experience is not unusual. They both shared this way with their men's and women's Bible studies, but they didn't share this way with each other.

Fellowship also implies mutual correction given with love and tenderness. Tim Keller suggests that we give our spouse a "hunting license," to bring correction when necessary. We should never use this license when angry. Rather, we should correct with compassion and gentleness. "Brothers, if anyone is caught in any transgression, you who are spiritual should restore him (or her) *in a spirit of gentleness*. Keep watch on yourself, lest you too be tempted" (Galatians 6:1).

Last, fellowship means identifying when and where God's grace is at work in your mate. God's grace is always at work. The key is noticing it.

"I was impressed with the way you disciplined our daughter yesterday. You were calm but determined."

"You are getting much better at resisting impulsive spending."

"Thank you for managing our finances. I don't take this for granted."

Married couples that practice fellowship with everyone but their spouse are missing out. Why? Because your spouse is the person closest to you. Your spouse is both the easiest, and at times the hardest, person to open up with. This means that your ability to deepen your friendship with your spouse might be an acid test of your spiritual maturity. Best friends work at fellowship. This is especially true of spouses.

In summary, we have discussed five foundations for healthy, vibrant marital friendship—shared goals, earned respect, acts of kindness and service, unhurried time alone together, and the regular practice of biblical fellowship.

CONCLUSION

Both Christians and non-Christians want marital intimacy, but for Christians it is never ultimate. That is because it can never provide what only God can give—*ultimate* meaning, purpose, and joy. But surprisingly, making God ultimate liberates us to really celebrate and deepen our relationship with our spouse. Cultivating marital friendship matters. It matters because it glorifies the relationship between Christ and his bride.

At the beginning of the last chapter we introduced Stan and Kate. The good news is that they are rebuilding their friendship. It's been challenging work, but they are willing, and they are making progress. They have a great future. Like Stan and Kate, there is great hope for all marriages willing to intentionally deepen their friendship with their spouse.

STUDY QUESTIONS

- Do you agree that your relationship with God is the necessary foundation for a growing friendship with your spouse? Why or why not?
- How would you make an argument that marital friendship matters to God?
- After reading this chapter, are there any biblical principles for building marital friendship about which you and your spouse do not agree? If so, discuss them. What can you do to agree?
- Are you tempted to make your spouse's approval more important than God's? Why or Why not?
- Do you practice biblical fellowship with your spouse? Why or why not?
- Are you in the habit of scheduling time together alone? If so describe. If not, why not?

THIRTEEN: God's Super Glue

I AM A BIG FAN OF SUPER GLUE. I use it to attach all kinds of things, and it usually works as advertised. It binds small things and big things. In fact, there is a video on YouTube showing a crane lifting a 5,000-pound pickup twenty feet into the air, and all that connects it is ten drops of Super Glue.

Sex has many purposes in marriage, but its most important might be its bonding power. It is God's relational Super Glue. It binds husband and wife socially, emotionally, and physically. In fact, this binding power is one reason that God forbids unmarried sex. "Or do you not know that he who is joined to a prostitute becomes *one body with her*? For, as it is written, "The two will become one flesh" (1 Corinthians 6:16). Here is a great mystery, and one we don't fully understand. The act of sex binds two people. The binding is more than physical. For this reason, married couples should engage in sex regularly and frequently.

In addition, your sexual relationship with your spouse is the one thing, besides the Ephesians five governmental order, that makes your relationship unique. That is not the case with the subjects of the previous chapters, i.e. humility and friendship. God commands humility in all human relationships. We develop friendships with many to whom we are not married. But Christians only engage in sexual intercourse with one person—their spouse. That means we should take a hard look at sex. What does a healthy sexual attitude look like? What is God's purpose for sex? What can couples do to improve their sexual relationship?

SEX MATTERS

God loves human sexuality. He created it, and designed it to bless marriage, but tragically, Christians don't always see it that way. We often underestimate its long-term value. Or, we do the opposite. We overemphasize its immediate importance while decoupling it from our spiritual life. Those who counsel marriages soon discover that sex between husbands and wives, in troubled marriages, is often rare or disappearing. When this happens, it is seldom because of physical inability. The problem is usually apathy resulting from relational stress. This is not God's plan. In the words of theologian, Denny Burk,

> Paul teaches not that couples *may* come together in regular conjugal union but that they *must* come together. Sexual intimacy is not merely a privilege of marriage but also a duty. Thus, sexual intimacy within marriage becomes a touchstone for the spiritual and emotional vitality of marriage.[1]

God is no prude. It pleased him greatly to give humanity the gift of sex. He created eroticism for his glory. Therefore, he is not ashamed of its pleasures and joys. If that is true, we shouldn't be either.

Think about this famous verse from Proverbs. "Rejoice in the wife of your youth, a lovely deer, a graceful doe. Let her breasts fill you at all times with delight; be intoxicated always in her love" (Proverbs 5:18–19). In fact, the subject of an entire Old Testament book, The Song of Songs, is primarily erotic love.

> Your stature is like a palm tree, and *your* breasts are like its clusters. I say I will climb the palm tree and lay hold of its fruit. Oh may your breasts be like clusters of the vine, and the scent of your breath like apples (Song of Solomon 7:7–8).

Because the Jews were a people of the Book, they had a healthy attitude towards sex. Sex was one of the three basic rights that a wife could expect from her husband. The other two were food and shelter. Husbands were obligated to fulfill these needs. In fact, a man's sexual duties to his wife were so important that the Mishnah (oral tradition of Jewish law) regulates their frequency. For example, a man who drives camels is required to perform his "onah" (sexual obligation) at least once a month, while a sailor is only obligated once every six months. The man not bound by work duties should give his wife her onah rights daily."[2] That's right. Daily!

It should not surprise us that God delights in human sexuality. He has imbedded the glory of sex throughout creation. Almost all living things are sexual. The God who created everything, with few exceptions, divided his creation into two sexes—male and female—even fruit trees. Male pollen must fertilize a female ovum before the apple tree can produce fruit.

All mammal species engage in elaborate courtship rituals resulting in copulation, pregnancy, and birth. Think of all the ways God could have arranged procreation but didn't. Creation could be sexless and passionless. Instead, erotic joy pervades

God's work of creation. When I was a boy I raised homing pigeons. I vividly remember their intricate wooing rituals. The cock would strut in circles around the oblivious, sometimes irritated, hen. Cooing loudly, he would bow, and scrape with his tail feathers spread out like a fan on the ground. The hen usually acted uninterested or irritated. Sometimes she would just walk away. But eventually he would get lucky. A hen would respond, and once mated they remained together for life.

Even though the Bible and creation teach that sex is God's plan, the church has not always seen it that way. We live in a fallen world, and human sexuality has been one of the victims.

CHANGING SEXUAL ATTITUDES

Augustine (AD 354-430) was the most influential early church father. By any measure, he was a great man. But like all great men he had flaws. One was his attitude toward sex. Prior to conversion he lived a promiscuous lifestyle. He kept a mistress with whom he had a son, Adeodatus (gift of God). In fact, fear that he wouldn't be able to give up casual sex delayed his conversion.

For this reason, after his conversion, he saw sexual temptation as the mother of all sins. His perspective on human sexuality was mostly negative, and because he was such an influential Christian thinker, his thinking cast a long shadow. For the next millennia Augustine's writings formed the church's theological backbone. This explains why some medieval theologians taught that when a married couple had sex the Holy Spirit left the room. It is also why Roman Catholics believe that Mary was a perpetual virgin.

Because the 16th century Reformation was a recovery of the Bible it was also a recovery of biblical attitudes about sexuality, specifically the joy and beauty of sex in marriage.

Martin Luther (1483-1546) was a monk and an Augustinian theologian. But when it came to sex in marriage, he rejected Augustine and embraced the Bible. As we have seen, in his early forties he shocked the 16th century world by marrying an ex-nun, Katie Von Bora. His recent biographer, Eric Metaxas, wrote that Luther saw his marriage as—

> An act of worship...countering the falsely pious antipathy to the physical, and specifically to the erotic. God had created the physical and the sexual as good, and he had redeemed them from their broken fallenness via marriage. Thus, not only was there nothing dirty about this, but the opposite was true. Luther thought unnatural celibacy to be of the Devil and natural and healthy marital sex to be something that glorified God.[3]

This was revolutionary thinking.

As we have already noted, because the 17th century Puritan movement was the high water of the Reformation, it was also the high water of a biblical view of sex in marriage. "Married sex," notes Leland Ryken, "was not only legitimate in the Puritan view; it was meant to be *exuberant*."[4] Ryken continues, for the Puritans "Sex...[was] part of a total union of two persons, including their minds, emotions, and souls as well as their bodies."[5] British historian, Antonia Fraser, writes that "It was a maxim of a popular Puritan handbook that 'the benefit of the bed' was one of the chief practical advantages to be expected from marriage."[6] In fact a 17th century New England Puritan congregation excommunicated a man because he refused to engage in sex with his wife.

C. J. Mahaney, speaking to husbands, sums this up for a contemporary audience.

> It is God's desire that every Christian couple, including you and your wife, regularly enjoy the best, most intimate, most satisfying sexual relations of which humans are capable. We're talking really, really good sex. Marital intimacy is God's gift to those who enter his holy covenant of marriage.[7]

Before we explore the beauty of marital sex further, we need to pause to examine its purposes, because God's reasons for sex go deeper than Super Glue.

God's Purpose for Sex

When we examine the Bible's teaching on sex we find at least four purposes—procreation, a defense against immorality, bonding/pleasure, and glory for God.

Procreation is obvious. On the sixth day of creation God said, "Let us make man in our image, after our likeness." Then, he commanded them to "Be fruitful and multiply and fill the earth and subdue it" (Genesis 1:26, 28). As we already noted in chapter one, "Image and likeness" are synonyms for God's moral glory. In other words, God commanded Adam and Eve to "multiply and fill the earth" with humans that reflected God's moral glory back to him. Ultimately, that is what parenting is all about. Marital sex was necessary to this task of filling the earth.

When an egg and sperm unite in a mother's womb a husband and wife participate with God in the creation of something *eternal*. What a privilege! The child will never die. It will live forever, either in heaven with God, or in eternal conscious torment in hell. This means that sex is an immense responsibility. The consequences are eternal! This is another reason that sex outside of marriage is such a great sin. A child growing up without its biological father (or mother) has a much smaller chance of obtaining the faith that leads to conversion. For this reason, God designed parenting to be a team sport.

A second purpose for marital sex was protection from immorality. It is interesting that the Roman Catholic Church, influenced by Augustine, thought that chastity meant virginity. But the Puritans, influenced by the Bible, thought that chastity meant *married* sex. Sex in marriage, not celibacy, is the biblical ideal of chastity. God created sexual desire, and then gave us marriage to satisfy and protect it. Marital chastity is what Paul had in mind when he wrote in his first letter to the Corinthians.

> But because of the temptation to sexual immorality, each man should have his own wife and each wife her own husband...To the unmarried and the widows, I say that it is good for them to remain single, as I am. But if they cannot exercise self-control, they should marry. For it is better to marry than to burn with passion (1 Corinthians 7:2, 8–9).

God gives very few the gift of celibacy. Everyone else will most likely "burn." Therefore, the vast majority of Christians should get married. If they don't, the "burning" will probably find a sinful outlet.

We have already noted the third reason for sex in marriage—bonding. Mutual pleasure is inherent to the glue that bonds. Referring to the Puritans, Leland Ryken, (quoted earlier) wrote, "The one-flesh relationship is the most intense, physical intimacy, and deepest, spiritual unity possible between a husband and wife."[8] We can sum up the Puritan view this way; marital sex is the most powerful way one human being can communicate love, care, and intimacy to another.

The truth that sex is communication should not surprise us. Throughout the Bible sex is referred to as "knowing" someone. "And Adam *knew* his wife, and she conceived and bore Cain" (Gen 4:1). "Joseph took his wife but *knew* her not until she had given birth to a son" (Matthew 1:25). The Greek word translated "knowing" is usually *ginosko*, a word that refers to experiential—as opposed to speculative—knowledge. I can "know" math speculatively, but I "know" my spouse experientially. God wants each husband and wife to "know" one another more deeply through the sex act. This "knowing" should get richer and deeper as the decades pass. One reason that God created sex to be pleasurable was to enhance this "knowing."

This bonding is most likely to occur when marital sex is regular and frequent. Christian marriage means the transfer of ownership of our body to our spouse. When the Corinthian church wrote Paul asking if they could get more sanctified by abstaining from marital sex, Paul surprised them.

> The husband should give to his wife her conjugal rights, and likewise the wife to her husband. For the wife does not have authority over her own body, but the husband does. Likewise, the husband does not have authority over his own body, but the wife does. Do not deprive one another, except perhaps by agreement for a limited time, that you may devote yourselves to prayer; but then come together again, so that Satan may not tempt you because of your lack of self-control (1 Corinthians 7:2–5).

In this passage Paul makes two points. First, neither husband or wife owns their body. When you marry you give your spouse the rights to your body. The context is sex. That doesn't mean you must engage in some sexual practice with which you are not comfortable. It means you shouldn't habitually defer with the excuse, "I'm too tired."

Second, except for special times devoted to prayer, Paul does not want couples to abstain from sex. In other words, he wants us to energetically protect and nourish this vital physical gift.

What "frequent" means will vary from couple to couple. It also varies by season of life. "Frequent" will be different for those in their twenties than those in their seventies. The Bible gives us great freedom here.

Sometimes sex is a duty. It is what a friend once called "routine married sex." You serve your spouse even though you don't feel like it. At other times sex is passionate. Both are normal marital experiences.

The bonding and communication that God wants us to experience is a byproduct of romance. You might be surprised to know that most cultures, throughout history, have not connected marriage with romantic passion. Romance was for extramarital affairs. In fact, it was those dull, boring, legalistic 17th century Puritans who changed this.

Looking at the marital model of passionate single-minded devotion described by Paul in Ephesians five, they took the next logical step—romance. In chapter one I quoted Edward Taylor, New England Puritan minister and poet, who wrote to his wife that his passion for her was a "golden ball of pure fire."[9] "The conversion of courtly love," observes C. S. Lewis, "into romantic monogamous love was...largely the work of English, and even of Puritan, poets...they created the new social institution of *romantic marriage*."[10]

The bonding power of sex is unique to human beings. Earlier we saw that God has salted his entire creation with sex. But for most other mammals, sex is purely functional. There is no bonding. Sex only occurs when the female is in heat. The goal is reproduction, and nothing more.

Humans are the only mammals for whom sex is about much more than reproduction. Human females don't go into heat. Therefore, humans mate year-round. This is unique, and it is God's doing. Because of its bonding power, God wants us to engage in sex year-round.

The fourth, and most important, reason for human sexuality is the glory of God. In his important book, *The Meaning of Sex*, Denny Burk, professor at Southern Seminary, writes,

> The ultimate purpose of sex is the glory of God. Sex, gender, marriage, manhood, womanhood— all of it— exist ultimately for the glory of God. The glory of God as the ultimate purpose of sex is not merely a theological deduction. It is the explicit teaching of Scripture.[11]

This means that when a husband and wife engage in sexual intercourse, the Holy Spirit doesn't leave the room. He is there rejoicing. Why? Because God created human sexuality for his glory, and he rejoices when we use it in a way that glorifies him. In his book on marriage, Christopher Ash writes,

> All of the people of God in the new heavens and new earth are the bride of Jesus Christ. That is to say, he loves them passionately, and they love him with an answering love. And in that new age their love will be consummated with an intimacy and enduring delight that the best human marriage can only begin faintly to echo. To put it bluntly, the most climactic and rapturous delight ever experienced in sexual intimacy by a married couple in the history of the human race cannot hold a candle to the delight of that union.[12]

GOOD MARRIAGES MAKE GOOD SEX

All of this begs the question, what can couples do to improve their sexual experience? After about five years of marriage I attended a seminar for couples on Christian marriage. I was in my late twenties. One of the breakout sessions was for men only, and the subject was sex. As you can imagine, it was well attended.

The speaker began with this question. "What is your wife's most sensitive sex organ?" The world answers body parts, techniques, sex toys, positions, etc. The men in the class answered accordingly, stressing one piece of anatomy or another, but the speaker just kept shaking his head. When we finally gave up, he said,

"It's her mind."

For me this was a revelation, and I don't think I was alone. Even though married for five years, I didn't really understand my wife, or what moved her sexually. Visual stimuli and touch arouse men. Although they can also arouse women, fundamentally, women respond differently. They respond to kindness, communication, the feeling of being appreciated, valued, and loved. That is why I put this chapter last. Their sexual response is very different from men. This means that good sex is a byproduct of the preceding chapters. *God has designed the female sexual response so that men can only get what they want when they treat their wife the way God wants.*

Good marriages, i.e. great friendships, make great sex. Great sex rarely makes a bad marriage good, but a good marriage will often make bad sex good. Here is the lesson for men. "Before you touch her body," writes C. J. Mahaney, "touch her mind."[13] Great social intercourse precedes great sexual intercourse.

In other words, great sex is a function of great love, i.e. great serving. The more a couple humbles themselves and serves each other the better their sexual relationship. The deeper a couple's friendship the greater their sexual relationship. Good sex is a fruit of the daily disciplines of serving, listening, forgiving, giving, and having fun together. That is how God designed it to work.

God created sex to reinforce the roles he created men and women to walk out. Therefore, sex is only apt to provide the satisfaction and joy that God intended when practiced in a lifetime relationship of mutual love and self-sacrifice, i.e. when we attempt to walk out Ephesians 5:22-33.

That is why the social sciences have discovered that the more "religious" a couple the greater their sexual satisfaction. Sex satisfies when we follow the Designer's manual—the Bible. You can promiscuously move from one relationship to another. The rewards will be temporary and fleeting at best. That is because God created us for something richer and more satisfying.

God engineered the female sexual response so that a husband must serve his wife to get the sexual joy that he wants. He has wired men such that women must respect, love, and encourage their leadership to get the security, relationship, and love that they want. Even secular social scientists understand this. "The determining factor in whether wives feel satisfied with the sex, romance, and passion in their marriage," concludes Dr. Gottman, "is by 70 percent, the quality of the couple's friendship. For men, the determining factor is, by 70 percent, the quality of the couple's friendship. So men and women come from the same planet after all."[14]

When we pursue the pleasure of our spouse in our sexual relationship, our sexual relationship satisfies. When we selfishly pursue pleasure for its own sake, sex never satisfies. It is like heroin. We go looking for increasingly greater stimulus to achieve the satisfaction for which we long. It terminates in perversions like sado-masochism, violent pornography, etc. But when our happiness comes from the joy of our spouse, the reward is not just physical. It is also emotional and relational. To the degree that we do sex unselfishly, normal, routine marital sex delivers the rewards God intended.

SEXUAL BROKENNESS

I have written this chapter for the average Christian couple, couples lacking any deep emotional scars from past sexual abuse. But many reading this have been deeply wounded by your own, or someone else's, sexual sin. At some level you are sexually broken.

The sins against God's plan for human sexuality are numerous. For example, incest, pedophilia, enslavement to masturbation, addiction to pornography, same-sex attraction, sexual dysphoria, abortion, adultery, and/or sexual promiscuity have afflicted many reading these paragraphs.

Therefore, as I conclude this chapter I need to make a qualification. For a person who is not sexually broken, working on humility, serving each other, and building your friendship will spark the normal sexual passions, but those with deep sexual scars may need additional help.

Maybe your parents taught you that sex is dirty, and you are struggling to get over it. Maybe you have strong guilt associations connected with sex making it is difficult for you to respond. Maybe you were very promiscuous before marriage, and in your mind sex is associated with guilt and negativity. It could be that you were sexually abused as a child, either by other children or by trusted adults, and now your sexual associations are all negative. Maybe you are a woman that men have used. Now you are incapable of trusting your husband. Maybe previous promiscuity makes it difficult for you to be satisfied with one man, or if a man, one woman.

This is especially important for women. Remember, the female's most erotic organ is her mind. What she thinks about sex will control her ability to respond.

If this is you, you may need additional help. You may need professional counseling. The best place to get it is from your local church. If it doesn't have skilled counselors with expertise in this area, get a referral from your pastor. The point is simple: don't give up. There is tremendous hope for healing in Christ.

CONCLUSION

God created sex for his glory. When a married couple celebrates their love with sexual intercourse, God and the angels also rejoice. Therefore, God wants married couples to engage in sex regularly and frequently.

Prior to the Reformation, before the centrality of the Bible was restored, Augustine's sexual negativity prevailed. With the recovery of the Bible, during the Reformation, that changed. It culminated in the 17th century Puritans who, because they knew they were for the glory of God, rejoiced in the beauty of romance and marital sex.

Sex in marriage has several purposes. First, it is for procreation. Second, it protects us from sexual immorality. Third, it is God's Super Glue—a wonderful source of pleasure bonding husband and wife. Most importantly, as we just noted, it is for the glory of God.

Good marriages make good sex. It doesn't work the other way around. The more we humble ourselves and serve, the more we work at our friendship, the more we communicate, pray together, and read the Bible together, the greater our sexual joy. Good social intercourse precedes good sexual intercourse.

Because sexual brokenness is everywhere, some will need counseling to overcome the guilt and negativities associated with past sexual experiences.

For the rest of us it is helpful to remember that our sexual relationship is not a sprint. It is a marathon. It is a decades long adventure filled with highs, lows, and long straight stretches. The fruits accrue to those who persevere in faithfulness to Christ and a life of serving each other.

It is my sincere hope and trust that you and your spouse will grow together and increasingly glorify God with your sexual relationship.

STUDY QUESTIONS

These questions are not for small group use. They are for you and your spouse to promote discussion in a confidential setting.

- On a scale of 1-10 how satisfied are you with our sexual relationship?
- If you knew I wouldn't get upset, how would you evaluate me as a lover? Where can I improve?
- What am I better at, being a parent to our children or being a lover to you? Why or why not?
- Do we spend enough time together alone?
- What one thing can I do to improve our sexual relationship?

FOURTEEN: God's Dump Truck

IF YOU ARE LIKE ME, you have finished this book thinking, "I don't measure up." I can be selfish, petulant, self-willed, sullen, slow to forgive, and full of self-pity. I am often proud and selfish, and I'm not always the friend I should be.

That's right. You don't measure up. In fact, you never will, and your condition is worse than you think. Jesus made that clear. He ended the Sermon on the Mount, already packed with impossible ethical requirements, with this coup d' grace. *"You must be perfect as your heavenly Father is perfect"* (Matthew 5:28).

None of us meet this standard, and in this life, we never will. None of us are perfect. We are needy sinners, and for our need God has provided a glorious solution—the gospel! It is God's dump truck. This truck bed is loaded with "yards" of grace, and he dumps it on everyone who believes the gospel and repents. God's amazing grace buries our sins and inadequacies out of sight. Here is how it works. Although we already discussed it in chapter five, I am going to repeat it, because we can never hear the Good News enough!

Your faith unites you with Christ. He was "perfect." When you believe the gospel, God imputes his perfections (righteousness) to you and me. And even though we sin and fail, God accepts us because he sees us as *righteous with the perfections of his Son*. This is wonderful news!

But your faith also unites you with Christ in his death. Your routine selfishness, snotty comments, idolatries, and arrogance deserve God's wrath, but Jesus went to the cross and there he took the punishment we all deserve. Jesus exhausted God's wrath. There is none left for you and me.

Last, your faith unites you with Christ in his resurrection. When he rose to new life, you and I did also. This means new birth—the Holy Spirit has come to indwell you. He is God's spotlight, and he always has the light pointed on Christ. What he especially illuminates is his cross. Why?

As we have seen, Christ's love for us, expressed by his death, motivates us. It inspires us to respond to God's magnificent, amazing grace. It re-orients the apathetic and passive to zealous service.

Christ's cross also paints a picture of "the breadth, and length, and height, and depth" of Christ's love that "surpasses knowledge" (Ephesians 3:18-19). To the degree that we see it, we will try to imitate it. The cross is God's tutorial. It shows every believer what a holy life (of love) looks like. Believers who want to know God's love will meditate on the cross.

Last, as we have mentioned, when we fail, which is often, the cross bathes us in amazing grace. Even though we fail repeatedly that grace keeps flowing to every repentant sinner who trusts by faith in these truths.

God's Dump Truck

This is how needy sinners, living in a Genesis 3 world, recover God's wonderful plan for marriage described in Genesis two. They live day and night in the shadow of the cross.

I want to close with the words of Ambrose Bierce, quoted in the introduction.

> Marriage is a Community consisting of a master, a mistress, and *two slaves*, making in all, one person.

This is what marriage in paradise looks like—a master and a mistress joyfully living as slaves coram deo (before the face of God). The result is intense spiritual, relational, and physical unity and joy.

Let's put our marriages on God's highway and spend the rest of our life returning to God's Genesis two paradise.

MARRIAGE IN PARADISE

Endnotes

INTRODUCTION
[1] Roland Bainton, *Here I Stand,* (New York: Abingdon-Cokesbury, 1950) chapter 17

[2] J. I. Packer, *A Quest for Godliness,* (Wheaton: Crossway, 1990), chapter 16

[3] See Abraham Kuyper, *Lectures on Calvinism,* (Peabody: MA: Hendrikson, 1898, reprint 2008), Lecture Three

[4] C. S. Lewis, *The Four Loves,* (New York: Harcourt, Brace, Jovanovich, 1960, reprinted 1991), pg. 105-06

[5] Matthew Haste," Marriage and Family in the Life of Andrew Fuller," *Southern Baptist Journal of Theology,* Feb. 8, 2014, pg. 28

[6] Carl Trueman, (2015-02-28). Luther on the Christian Life: Cross and Freedom (Theologians on the Christian Life) (p. 187). Crossway. Kindle Edition.

[7] Ray Ortlund Jr., *Marriage and the Mystery of the Gospel* (p. 24). Crossway. Kindle Edition.

CHAPTER ONE
[1] Conger, Cristen, "Are married people happier than singles?" 01 June 2009, How Stuff Works.com
http://science.howstuffworks.com/life/married-people-happier-than-singles.htm

[2] http://www.evanmarckatz.com/blog/marriage/why-married-women-are-happier-than-single-women/

[3] http://family-studies.org/how-strong-families-help-create-prosperous-states/?utm_source=IFS+Main+List&utm_campaign=32b7a47f24-newsletter_103&utm_medium

=email&utmterm=0_c06b05f1ff-32b7a47f24-138499557

[4] Tim Keller: *The Meaning of Marriage,* (New York: Dutton, 2011) pg. 24

[5] http://www.evanmarckatz.com/blog/marriage/why-married-women-are-happier-than-single-women/ Also note a study done by the Department of Health and Human Services concluding that "Results from a study of 97 couples in a Midwestern metropolitan area suggest that joint participation in religious activities is associated with better marital functioning, greater marital satisfaction, more perceived personal benefit from marriage, less marital conflict, and greater use of collaboration for wives and husbands (Mahoney, et al., 1999). Higher levels of parental religiosity among 90 African American adolescents and their married parents in the rural South were associated with increased marital interaction, quality and support, and lower levels of conflict (Brody, Stoneman, Flor, & McCrary, 1994)." http://aspe.hhs.gov/hsp/08/relationshipstrengths/LitRev/index.shtml#Religion

[6] http://www.ccaa.net.au/documents/LITREVIEWJohnBennett.pdf , pg. 5

[7] Shaunti Feldhahn *The Good News About Marriage,* (Sisters OR: Multnomah, 2014) Pg. 86

[8] Leland Ryken, *Worldly Saints,* (Grand Rapids: Zondervan, 1986) pg. 39-40

[9] Erroll Hulse, *Who are the Puritans,* (Auburn, MA: Evangelical, 2000) pg. 140

[10] Roland Bainton, *Here I Stand,* (New York: Abingdon-Cokesbury, 1950), pg. 302

[11] Ibid Ryken, pg. 50

[12] Tim Keller quoting Robert Bellah's *Habits of the Heart* in *The Reason for God,* (New York, Dutton, 2008) pg. 69-70

[13] Quoted by Tim Keller, *The Meaning of Marriage,* (New York: Dutton, 2011) pg..27

[14] Burk, Denny (2013-10-31). What Is the Meaning of Sex? (Kindle Locations 1505-1506). Crossway. Kindle Edition.

[15] For more on this idea see Hoekema, Anthony, *Created In God's Image,* (Grand Rapids: Eerdmans, 1986)

[16] See Burk, Denny, *What Is The Meaning of Sex?* (Wheaton: Crossway, 2013), Chapter six

[17] Nancy Gibbs with Andréa Ford and Deirdre van Dyk, "What Women Want Now", *Time Magazine,* http://www.time.com/time/specials/packages/article/0,28804,1930277_1930145_1930309-2,00.html#ixzz0WDhmgrRL Nov 7, 2009

CHAPTER TWO

[1] Dr. Leonard Sax, *Why Gender Matters,* (New York: Broadway Books, 2005) pg. 5

[2] Dr. Larry Crabb, Quoted in John Piper and Wayne Grudem, *50 Crucial Questions,* (Louisville: CBMW, 1992), pg. 11

[3] This is not her real name.

[4] J. I. Packer, *Knowing God*, Chapter Five, electronic ed. (Downers Grove: InterVarsity, 1973).

[5] Also see (Ps 10:14, 30:10, 54:4, 118:7)

[6] George Gilder quotes a Hunter study, "Women have about 67% of the endurance of 55 % of the muscular strength of men. Even when size is held constant, women are only 80% as strong as men." He goes on...An Army study conducted at West Point showed that young women improve their strength less than half

as much as men under the same regimen of physical training." *Men and Marriage,* (Gretna: Pelican, 1986) pg. 132-33

[7] Phillip Longman, *The Empty Cradle,* (New York: Basic, 2004) pg. 2; Also see the DVD *Demographic Winter, The Sustainable Demographic Dividend,* an International Report from the Social Trends Institute, Sponsored by the National Marriage Project, Charlottesville, VA.

[8] See my book, *Gospel Powered Parenting,* (Phillipsburg: P&R, 2010)

[9] For more on this proposal read Fred Pearce, *The Coming Population Crash,* (Boston: Beacon Press, 2010). Especially chapters six and eight.

[10] Ibid, Longman, pg. 30-35

[11] Ibid, Longman

[12] Philip Longman, *The Empty Cradle,* (New York: Basic Books, 2004) pg. 15-18

[13] Philip Longman, "The Return of Patriarchy," *Foreign Policy,* Feb 17, 2006, Online Edition. Longman courageously labels the male investment in the family, "patriarchy."

[14] Charles Murray, *coming Apart,* (New York: Random House, 2012) chapter 8 "Marriage".

CHAPTER THREE
[1] This story is a synthesis of the lives of several couples with whom I am familiar.

CHAPTER FOUR
[2] Crossway Bibles, *The ESV Study Bible,* 56 (Wheaton, IL: Crossway Bibles, 2008).

[1] John Piper, *Brothers We Are Not Professionals,* (Nashville: Broadman & Holman, 2002), pg. 252

[2] Andreas Kostenberger: *God, Marriage, and Family,* (Wheaton: Crossway, 2004) pg. 62

[3] Ortlund Jr., Raymond C.. Marriage and the Mystery of the Gospel (p. 93). Crossway. Kindle Edition.

[4] Civil Authority (Rom. 13:1-7, 1 Pet. 2:13-17, 1 Thes. 5:12), submission by children to parents (Ex 20:12, Eph. 6:1-4, Col. 3:20-21), submission by church members to elders and pastors (1 Pet. 5:5, Heb. 13:17), submission by slaves to masters (Eph. 6:5-9, Col. 3:22-25, 1 Pet. 2:18, Titus 2:9-10, 1 Tim. 6:1-2), and by extension submission of employees to employers.

[5] D. M. Lloyd Jones, *Christian Marriage,* (Edinburgh: Banner of Truth, 1973) pg. 29

[6] Andreas Kostenberger: *God, Marriage, and Family,* (Wheaton: Crossway, 2004) pg. 62

[7] Ibid, D. M. Lloyd Jones, pg. 59

CHAPTER FIVE
[1] Texts which speak to God's moral standard—Hebrews 7:11, 19, 10:14, 12:23, Gal 5:2-3, James 2:10, Matthew 5:48.

[2] J.I. Packer, *Knowing God,* (Downers Grove: IVP, 1973), *Chap 13*

[3] R. C. Sproul, *The Truth of the Cross,* (Orlando, Reformation Trust, 2007), pg. 19 (italics mine).

[4] Dave Harvey, *Rescuing Ambition,* (Wheaton: Crossway, 2010), pg. 104

CHAPTER SIX
[1] Geisler, N. L., *Baker encyclopedia of Christian apologetics* (Grand Rapids, MI: Baker Books,1999) pg. 369

[2] Bruce Ware; *God's Greater Glory,* (Wheaton: Crossway, 2004), pg. 49 (Emphasis mine).

³ Charnock, Stephen. Christ Crucified (Vintage Puritan) (Kindle Locations 319-321). GLH Publishing. Kindle Edition.

CHAPTER SEVEN

¹ Ibid, Bainton, pg. 298

² Ibid, Bainton, pg. 289

³ Sproul, R.C.; Nichols, Stephen J.; Beeke, Joel R.; Calhoun, David B.; Denlinger, Aaron Clay; Ferguson, Sinclair B.; Godfrey, W. Robert; Horton, Michael S.; Lawson, Steven J.; Lucas, Sean Michael; MacArthur, John; Manetsch, Scott M.; Nichols, Stephen J.; Thomas, Derek W.H.; Veith, Gene Edward; Waters, Guy Prentiss; Yount, Terry. The Legacy of Luther (Kindle Locations 2069-2071). Ligonier Ministries, Inc. - USA. Kindle Edition.

⁴ Ibid, Bainton, page 301

⁵ Gary Thomas, *Sacred Marriage* ((Grand Rapids: Zondervan, 2000) pg. 13, italics mine.

⁶ Ibid, Gary Thomas, pg. 40

⁷ *The Works of Jonathan Edwards,* Vol 1, "Religious Affections," (Edinburgh: Banner of Truth, 1834, reprinted 1984) pg. 294, italics mine.

⁸ Sexting is when young women flirt with boys by sending them naked or half naked pictures of themselves.

CHAPTER EIGHT

¹ *The City of God,* Bk. 14, Chap. 13, Vol. 2 in *Nicene and Post-Nicene Fathers,* First Series (rpt.; Grand Rapids: Eerdmans, 1983), pg. 273

² Anthony Hoekema, *Created In God's Image,* (Grand Rapids: Eerdmans, 1986) pg. 173

³ See Tim Keller, *The Freedom of Self Forgetfulness.*

⁴ C. S. Lewis, *Mere Christianity,* New York: MacMillan, 1952), pg. 114

⁵ *The Works of Jonathan Edwards,* Vol 1, (Edinburgh: Banner of Truth, 1834, repub. 1984) pg. 300-301

⁶ Jones and Fontenot, *The Prideful Souls Guide to Humility* (Billerica MA. DPI, 2003) pg. 92, emphasis mine.

CHAPTER NINE

¹ There are different interpretations of Isaiah 14 as a description of Satan's fall. So, if you hold otherwise, no problem. However, I concur with Wayne Grudem, who in his *Systematic Theology* writes, "It is also possible that there is a reference to the fall of Satan, the prince of demons, in Isaiah 14. As Isaiah is describing the judgment of God on the king of Babylon (an earthly, human king), he then comes to a section where he begins to use language that *seems too strong to refer to any merely human king*" (Grand Rapids: Zondervan, 1994, pg. 413). I agree with Grudem for several reasons. First, it is not unusual for prophets to jump from an earthly to heavenly reference in the middle of an extended prophecy (2 Sam 7:12-17, Ezek. 28:11-19). Second, other texts in the Bible seem to suggest that demons are organized in a hierarchy over political entities. For example, Daniel 10:12-14 describes a spiritual being who is "the prince of Persia." Paul refers to them as "thrones, dominions, rulers, or authorities" (Col. 1:16). Remember, Jesus called Satan the "Prince of this world" Therefore, it should not surprise us that Isaiah would address the "Prince of Babylon," the spiritual ruler of a political entity that symbolizes the world, with similar language.

² Kirsten Birket, *The Essence of Feminism,* (Kingsford: Matthias Media, 2000) pg. 99

³ McIlhaney Jr., MD, Joe; MD, Jennifer A. Shuford (2011-12-20). Girls Uncovered: New Research on What America's Sexual

Culture Does to Young Women (p. 13). Moody Publishers. Kindle Edition. (Italics Mine).

⁴ Dave Harvey, *Rescuing Ambition,* (Wheaton: Crossway, 2010) pg. 105-06

⁵ See Aida Donald, *Lion In The Whitehouse,* (New York: Basic Books, 2007), Chapter Four

CHAPTER TEN

¹ Also See Matthew 18:21-35 where Jesus tells the parable of the unforgiving servant. The unforgiving servant is not forgiven because he refuses to forgive.

² Andre Seu, *World Magazine,* "The Thing We Won't Do," Sept 30, 2006

³ John M. Gottman, Ph. D., *Seven Principles For Making Marriage Work,* (New York: Three Rivers Press, 1999) pg. 29

⁴ Marc Theissen: "America is on its way to divorce court," Fox News 6/24/17.

ʷwww.challies.com citing USA Today "This Might Be The Key To a Happy Marriage," Oct. 24, 2015

⁶ *Dictionary of Paul and His Letters,* edited by Hawthorne, Martin, and Reid, "Benediction, Blessing, Doxology, Thanksgiving," Peter Obrien (Downers Grove, IVP, 1993), pg. 69

⁷ C.J. Mahaney, Humility: *True Greatness,* pg. 71 (Sisters, OR, Multnomah, 2005)

⁸ Ray Ortlund Jr. *When God Comes to Church,* (Grand Rapids, Baker, 2000), pg. 200

⁹ Andrew Murray, *Humility,* (Feather Trail Press, 2009) pg. 14-15

CHAPTER ELEVEN

¹ Ibid, Gottman, pg. 19-20, italics mine.

² Tripp, Paul David. *What Did You Expect? Redeeming the Realities of Marriage* (p. 56). Crossway. Kindle Edition. Italics mine.

CHAPTER TWELVE

¹ Quoted by J. I. Packer in *A Quest for Godliness,* (Wheaton: Crossway, 1990) pg. 260

² Trueman, Carl R. (2015-02-28). Luther on the Christian Life: Cross and Freedom (Theologians on the Christian Life) (p. 185). Crossway. Kindle Edition.

³ Ibid, Packer, pg. 262

⁴ F. Bradford Wilcox, "The Evolution of Divorce," Issue 1, 2009, *National Affairs.* Italics mine.

⁵ Ibid., Keller, pg. 78, italics mine.

⁶ See Dr. Leonard Sax *Boys Adrift* (New York: Basic Books) and *Why Gender Matters?* (New York: Random House, 2017)

⁷ My book, *Gospel Powered Parenting,* (Philipsburg: P&R, 2009) might prove helpful.

⁸ DeWitt, Steve (2012-03-01). *Eyes Wide Open* (p. 129). Credo House Publishers. Kindle Edition. Quoting C.S. Lewis, *God in the Dock,* (Grand Rapids: Eerdmans, 1970) pg 280

⁹ Tripp, Paul David. *What Did You Expect?* Redeeming the Realities of Marriage (p. 52). Crossway. Kindle Edition.

¹⁰ J. I Packer, *Eighteen Words,* (Ross-Shire Scotland: Christian Focus, 1981) pg. 186-87

CHAPTER THIRTEEN

¹ Burk, Denny. *What Is the Meaning of Sex?* (Kindle Locations 2049-2051). Crossway. Kindle Edition. (italics mine).

²http://www.mesacc.edu/~thoqh49081/StudentPapers/JewishSexuality.html

[3] Eric Metaxas, *Martin Luther,* (New York: Viking, 2017), pg. 342

[4] Ibid, Ryken, pg. 44 (italics mine).

[5] Ibid, Ryken, pg. 45

[6] Antonia Fraser, quoting the Puritan Daniel Rogers in *Cromwell The Lord Protector,* (New York: Knopf, 1973) pg. 28

[7] C. J. Mahaney, *Sex, Romance, and the Glory of God,* (Wheaton: Crossway, 2004) pg. 15

[8] Ibid, Mahaney quoting Daniel L. Akin, "Sermon: The Beauty and Blessings of the Christian Bedroom" *The Southern Baptist Journal of Theology,* Vol 6, No. 1, Spring 2002, pg. 94

[9] Ibid Ryken, pg. 50

[10] Ibid, Ryken, pg. 51

[11] Burk, Denny. *What Is the Meaning of Sex?* (Kindle Locations 313-315). Crossway. Kindle Edition.

12. Christopher Ash (2007-07-01). *Married for God* (Kindle Locations 2003-2006). Intervarsity Press. Kindle Edition.

[13] Ibid, Mahaney, pg. 58

[14] Ibid, Gottman, pg. 17

Made in the USA
Columbia, SC
07 November 2024